WAKEFULNESS AND WORLD

■

"An invitation to philosophy in the strongest sense. Through a patient and elegant discussion of some key moments in classic texts from Plato, Aristotle, Kant, and Hegel, Linck invites his readers to wake up to the strangeness and miraculousness which is the making intelligible of the world in thought." —Louis Colombo, Associate Professor of Philosophy, Bethune-Cookman University

"This project is an introduction to philosophy in the way that having a discussion with the finest teachers of philosophy is rumored to have been: Wittgenstein puzzling out utterances; Aristotle on peripatetic garden walks; and Socrates, whose every illustration proved both familiar and unsettling. In *Wakefulness and World*, Linck speaks directly to beginners as well as practiced scholars about our endeavors to understand, from the images that lure us into reflection, to the confrontation between intelligible generalization and everyday experience. Linck's book brings us into conversation with Plato's Socrates, with Aristotle, Kant, Hegel, and with Newton. Through these encounters, he guides the reader into a profound reckoning with the conditions that allow careful, critical inquiry to flourish." —Katie Terezakis, Professor of Philosophy, Rochester Institute of Technology

"The subject of this slim and lucid volume is the wondrous intelligibility of experience as it comes to light through philosophical attentiveness to the world. Linck moves from the tentative hypotheses of Plato's Socrates, to Aristotle's elucidation of the determinateness of natural and artificial beings, to Kant's and Hegel's astonishing explorations of the ways the world's intelligibility arises from within the mind itself. A deeply intelligent and subtle book by a master reader and teacher, *Wakefulness an[d World]* inform educated amateurs and accom[plished] —Jacob Howland, author of *The Rep[ublic... Phi]losophy* and *Glaucon's Fate*

"*Wakefulness and World* invites readers into a brief history of Western Philosophy through close readings of Plato, Aristotle, and Kant. More importantly, through a series of imagination exercises, it urges us to reconsider seemingly ordinary acts: what it means to see, to speak, and to count, reigniting early childhood experiences of astonishment at the very fact of being in the world. Each chapter provides foundational lessons in how to read (another person, a text, a statement, a scene, a concept, a swarm). Rather than outline a familiar philosophical trajectory from the sensible to the intelligible, Linck stages their entanglement and shows the urgency of returning to topics (and figures) that deepen through renewed contact. If philosophy is a never-ending project of awakening, *Wakefulness and World* leaves one feeling newly alert to the ongoing project of philosophizing, as well as freshly alive to 'the astonishing space of intelligible luminosity that we call the world.'" —Megan Craig, Associate Professor of Philosophy and Art, Stony Brook University

WAKEFULNESS

and

WORLD

AN INVITATION TO PHILOSOPHY

■

Matthew Linck

PAUL DRY BOOKS
Philadelphia 2019

First Paul Dry Books Edition, 2019

Paul Dry Books, Inc.
Philadelphia, Pennsylvania
www.pauldrybooks.com

Printed in the United States of America

ISBN: 978-1-58988-136-5

CONTENTS

A NOTE TO THE READER

The chapters in this book are an attempt to say something about philosophy, about the endeavor of philosophizing. This attempt is approached differently in the different chapters. In the first, a search is undertaken to find a picture of philosophy. In the second, a question is asked about how to begin in philosophy and what it looks like to set out from that beginning. The third chapter strives above all to get swept up in a movement of thought by taking on a particular question. The last chapter attempts to enact the unsettling force of philosophical effort.

In each case, the chapters scrutinize, reflect on, untangle or imitate certain classical philosophical texts. The book proceeds in this way from the conviction that reading such books is itself a way of philosophizing. The attempt to speak about philosophy undertaken here is not ultimately separable from an attempt to read these texts. But above all, speaking about and reading are in the service of an attempt to think.

Hence it is my wish not so much to speak to as read along with, and thereby think together with, the reader.

UNDERSTANDING, COMPREHENSION, INSIGHT—an intellect at work—is our common condition. Whenever we say, "These things belong together," we understand something, for we discern a common feature among these many things. So, too, is the intellect at work when we say, "That thing is different from this one." A sense of how things both hang together and stand apart is just the sense of a creature that orients itself by understanding.

We experience things hanging together and standing apart, but we can also catch sight of ourselves having this experience. Then we might want to know what makes it possible. How are we able to sense that things hang together and stand apart—that there is order and intelligibility in the world? What is responsible for our sense that things can be grouped by kind because we see them as the same or set apart because we see them as different? Is our experience of how the world shows itself underwritten by principles?

If an active mind is our common condition, mathematics offers us a uniquely cleared-out space in which to see the intellect at work. The experience of proving theorems, the clarity of discernment in geometrical reasoning, and the necessity encountered when operating with numbers—all of these demand our assent that something is *just so* and that we have understood something. Is, though, the experience of intelligibility in mathematics the same as worldly comprehension? Can success in mathematical reasoning stand in for what successful comprehension would be in general? Does the experience of mathematical necessity carry with it an understanding of how that experience is possible, or must we look for that understanding outside of mathematics?

An intellect at work is an intellect that knows—or at least claims to know. An intellect that claims to know has an understanding of what makes it possible to know. When knowledge is accompanied by certainty, the knower will always have an answer to the question, "*How* do you know?" For the knower, the answer to this question will be an attempt to stamp its certainty with the mark of truth. But does this make it so? Can we trust that knowing with certainty is knowing truly? Can we trust that *we* truly know when we are certain we know something? What if we find that our certain knowledge fails to hold the stamp of truth? What then?

WAKEFULNESS and WORLD

WAKEFULNESS

To find a picture of philosophy.

AT THE MIDPOINT of Plato's *Republic*, Socrates provides a definition of the philosopher. He says that philosophers are "lovers of the sight of the truth" (475e). Socrates' young companion Glaucon agrees, but wants to hear more about what Socrates means by his assertion. Socrates anticipates that his attempt to elaborate on his definition will go more easily with Glaucon than it might with someone else. Let's listen in to the next bit of their conversation.[1]

"It wouldn't be at all easy to tell someone else. But you, I suppose, will grant me this."

"What?"

"Since beautiful is opposite to ugly, they are two."

"Of course."

"Since they are two, isn't each also one?"

"That is so as well."

"The same argument also applies then to justice and injustice, good and bad, and all the forms [*eide*]; each is itself one, but, by showing themselves every-

> where in a community with actions, bodies, and one
> another, each looks like many."
>
> "What you say," he said, "is right." (475e–476a)

There is no discussion here about what a form, *eidos*, is.
Glaucon, it seems, is either familiar with this way of talking
or understands on the spot what Socrates means. In some
respects, it is not such a strange way of speaking. *Eidos* is an
ordinary Greek word, typically indicating a class or kind
of thing. Indeed, Glaucon is the first person to utter the
word in the *Republic* and he uses it in this sense.[2] The word
can be traced back to *horaō*, meaning to see. An *eidos* is the
"look" of a thing. Things with a common look fall into the
same class or kind.

Socrates regards these looks as somehow separate from
things (actions and bodies). Beauty, ugliness, justice, injustice, good, and bad: each, Socrates claims, is one. A man
performs a beautiful deed and you behold a beautiful vista.
The deed and vista are two, but beauty itself is one. It only
appears to be many as seen in the deed and the vista. One
and the same form of the beautiful *shows up* in many things.

THIS IS HOW things look to the philosopher. The philosopher sees, and takes delight in seeing, the singular forms as
they show themselves in the world. How, in Socrates' opinion, does the philosopher differ from one who does not see
forms? His conversation with Glaucon continues:

> "Well, now," I said, "this is how I separate them[3]
> out. On one side I put those of whom you were just
> speaking, the lovers of sights, the lovers of arts, and the
> practical men; on the other, those whom the argument
> concerns, whom alone are called philosophers."
>
> "How do you mean?" he said.

"The lovers of hearing and the lovers of sights, on the one hand," I said, "surely delight in beautiful sounds and colors and shapes and all that craft makes from such things, but their thought [*dianoia*] is unable to see and delight in the nature of the beautiful itself."

"That," he said, "is certainly so."

"Wouldn't, on the other hand, those who are able to approach the beautiful itself and see it by itself be rare?"

"Indeed they would."

"Is the man who holds that there are beautiful things but doesn't hold that there is beauty itself and who, if someone leads him to the knowledge of it, isn't able to follow—is he, in your opinion, living in a dream or is he awake? Consider it. Doesn't dreaming, whether one is asleep or awake, consist in believing a likeness of something to be not a likeness, but rather the thing itself to which it is like?"

"I, at least," he said, "would say that a man who does that dreams."

"And what about the man who, contrary to this, believes that there is something beautiful itself and is able to catch sight both of it and of what participates in it, and doesn't believe that what participates is it itself, nor that it itself is what participates—is he, in your opinion, living in a dream or is he awake?"

"He's quite awake," he said. (476a–d)

There is no way, based on these exchanges between Socrates and Glaucon, to determine if they are right about all of this! Glaucon goes along with everything we would want to question, most especially the presumption that there *are* forms to begin with.

But our goal in listening in to this conversation is not to determine whether the philosopher sees something really there in seeing forms. We are searching only for a picture of philosophy and the philosopher. Given that delight in form-seeing is the defining mark of the philosopher, what follows?

IMAGINE THAT YOU are reminiscing about a recent trip taken abroad. For a few moments your attention is fully absorbed in memories of a marvelous hike on a mountain path. Barely aware of your immediate surroundings, your memories become vivid, lifelike. It is as if you are back on the mountain. You are daydreaming. Then something nearby begins to grab your attention. For a brief moment you find yourself between two worlds. The vividness of the daydream lingers even as you start to register your immediate surroundings. It is at this moment that you are able to discern, in one moment, the difference between the daydream and what is real.

The philosopher is like one coming out of a daydream, catching sight both of what truly is and what "participates in it."

It is the "opinion" of Socrates and Glaucon that the philosopher "believes" that there are forms. The things said here about the philosopher follow an if/then line of reasoning. *If* there are forms as the philosopher believes—and he believes this because he sees them—then the philosopher is as one who is awake, one who is not taking phantoms as the things themselves.

UNDERSTOOD IN THIS WAY, philosophy is not premised on proving that there are forms. Philosophy begins with seeing the forms.

Socrates says that for the non-philosophers "their *thought* is unable to see and delight in" the forms. Form-seeing is a kind of thinking. To see forms among actions and bodies, then, is to take the world as double. The world shows itself in two ways to the philosopher, as sensible and as intelligible. Intelligible things show up in the sensible world.

Philosophy does not begin by proposing this distinction between the sensible and the intelligible. Philosophy has begun anywhere someone believes he has caught a glimpse of intelligible principles in the world.

THE DIFFERENCE between the sensible and the intelligible is not a piece of dogma for the philosopher. On Socrates' construal, the world shows *itself* as sensible and intelligible *to* the philosopher. Any talk that the philosopher engages in regarding this distinction is a response to seeing the world show itself in this way.

This means also that the philosopher does not regard the forms merely as a hypothesis. As pictured here, the philosopher is marked by having this peculiar experience. Forms are not supposed.

AS AN ACT of the intellect, form-seeing is a kind of knowing. It is not propositional knowledge, the sort that expresses itself in statements of the form "X is Y." Form-seeing for Socrates is a kind of knowing, it seems, because it is a vision of what is responsible for things being the way they are. It is this that makes it "sight of the truth." To say "The man's action was just" is to attach justice to the man's action. In saying this, one asserts knowledge of the justness of the action. In attesting to seeing justice itself as it shows up among many actions, one asserts a different kind of knowledge—not knowledge *that* this or that thing is just, but knowledge of *what* the ground of something being just is. Rather than statements such as "The man's action was just," form-seeing issues in statements such as "Just actions are just because they partake of justice itself." But as a kind of knowing, form-seeing is not itself captured in statements of this kind. Such a statement is premised on "knowing" the form already, on already having seen it.[4]

PHILOSOPHERS TRAFFIC in certain fundamental categories: being, becoming, and nothing; knowledge, opinion, and ignorance. Form-seeing itself necessitates the delineation of these categories. If form-seeing is knowing, it must be a knowing of something that *is*. And since the forms show themselves as singularly one—each one thing and nothing else—they exemplify being. Socrates says, "[W]hat *is* entirely, is entirely knowable" (477a). In contrast ignorance—lack of knowledge—depends on "what in no way *is*, [that which] is in every way unknowable."

Socrates and Glaucon proceed to locate opinion as falling between knowledge and ignorance. They agree that opinion names something having less clarity than knowledge, but not possessing the same degree of obscurity as ignorance. Their reasoning pushes them to assign what they call "the opinable" to opinion, since neither "what *is* entirely" nor "what in no way *is*" seems to correspond to opinion in the way it falls between knowledge and ignorance. "The opinable" is not an ordinary notion, but we will have occasion below to think of it as becoming.

UNFOLDING THESE implications of form-seeing leads to a certain picture of conscious-being-in-the-world. Engaging with the world in its becoming—the world in flux and undergoing change—is to engage in it through opinion. To achieve knowledge from within the world would require discerning what *is* within the flux of becoming. And to avoid ignorance would require—somehow—to avoid taking what is not for what is.

BUT HOW DO we know that the philosopher is not simply mistaken in thinking he has seen forms? Might it not be a kind of hallucination?

The beginnings of an answer come near the end of this portion of the conversation. Socrates suggests to Glaucon that for those who do not believe that there are forms, nothing will look just one way to them. A beautiful thing will also, in some respect or some circumstance, appear ugly. Something appearing just will also appear unjust. And so forth. Socrates asks, "Then is each of the several manys [i.e., ordinary sensible things] what one asserts it to be any more than it is not what one asserts it to be?" (479b). That is, if ordinary things can look one way and another, is our speech and thought capable of capturing them? Is meaningful thought and speech at all possible if all that exists are the variously appearing "manys"? That is, is there any *being* within becoming? Glaucon gets it just right, I think, when he responds by saying, "the manys are [. . .] ambiguous, and it's not possible to think of them fixedly as either being or not being, or as both or neither" (479c). Hence, it turns out that the experience of form-seeing raises the question of what happens in speech and thought. Are our speaking and thinking *about* something determinate? If the "manys" turn out not to be "fixed" and we do think our speech and thought can attain determination, then there must be something that grounds that attainment. Meaningful speech and thought depend on there being determinate things. The two stand or fall together. But the philosopher, as the one who starts from a vision of the forms among sensible things, is in no position to simply assert that it is so, that speech and thought and being have determinacy because there are forms. All he can say is that it *looks* that way to him.

WAKEFULNESS IS the condition of the philosopher *if* there are forms.

■

Is Socrates a philosopher? Given the way he defines the philosopher in Book V of the *Republic*, it is not immediately clear. Plato neither shows us nor has Socrates report about episodes of form-seeing. The forms are sometimes a topic of discussion (especially in *Parmenides*, *Symposium*, and *Phaedo*), and as we will eventually see, Socrates often asks his companions to speak about some matter *in terms of* a single form, but this is not the same as seeing forms.

The most obvious thing to say about Socrates is that he is a talker. Plato's dialogues are imitations of conversations. If we can grasp the nature and goal of the conversations that Socrates engages in, perhaps we can connect his activity in conversation with the notion of the philosopher as a seer of forms.

We begin by considering a portion of Plato's *Gorgias*, the portion in which Socrates talks with Polus. This portion of this particular dialogue will serve as an emblem of twin features of Socratic conversation: that it is a common endeavor and that it aims at truth.

Some context is needed. *Gorgias* begins as do many dialogues, with Socrates arriving in the middle or at the end of some conversation, only to begin a new one. In this case, Socrates arrives at the home of an Athenian who is hosting the visiting Gorgias and his young associate, Polus. Callicles informs Socrates that he has missed a formidable display of rhetorical art given by Gorgias. The opening exchanges of the dialogue lead Socrates to inquire, with Gorgias, into the nature of rhetoric. This conversation exposes a problem for the teacher of rhetoric, namely, that he claims to know what justice is but disclaims responsibility for any unjust use that his students may make of rhetorical art. That is, despite his knowledge of what justice is, the teacher of rhetoric is not responsible for making his students just. There is a lack of harmony here that Socrates cannot abide.

At this point Polus interrupts the conversation. His interjection is centered on two claims. He says that the path of the conversation taken by Socrates and Gorgias arose from Gorgias not being willing to admit that the teacher of rhetoric might not know what justice is or that he might not teach it to the student who came to him ignorant of this. Polus then suggests that there is something false or artificial about the preceding conversation since it was not based on the genuine views held by the speakers. Even if what preceded made sense, it was still false because some of its premises were false. Additionally, Polus accuses Socrates of doing this on purpose, leading the conversation in such a way that Gorgias would have to say things he did not believe (because it would be shameful publicly to utter his true views), and in this way Socrates would be able to make Gorgias contradict himself. "Just what you love (461c)," Polus says to Socrates.[5]

IT IS A MARK of his good nature that Polus goes on to talk with Socrates at some length. Polus may want to show that he can avoid Socrates' traps, that he can prove himself by putting himself in Socrates' way. Nevertheless, Polus seems genuinely to desire to talk with Socrates. This goodwill is a crucial element in what unfolds.

Socrates persuades Polus to join him in a conversation of short questions and answers, but when Polus does not understand what Socrates says about rhetoric being a form of pandering, Socrates gives a long speech in which he lays out a series of analogies. The gist of Socrates' proposal is that rhetoric looks as if it is the art of politics, but operates with a knack for persuading rather than through knowledge of what is best. Socrates offers two analogies. Rhetoric stands to politics as cooking stands to medicine, and as cosmetics stands to gymnastic training. That is, cooking is a knack for making the body feel good, whereas medicine is an art based on knowledge that makes the body healthy; and cosmetics is a knack for making the body appear beautiful, whereas gymnastic training in fact makes the body beautiful.

Polus rightly understands that Socrates is criticizing rhetoricians. The charge of pandering cuts deeply. It is another mark of Polus' good nature that he does not get defensive at this point. He asks instead what seems to be a sincere question: Don't the rhetoricians have the greatest power in their cities (through the power of persuasion)? Socrates responds to this question by tracing out a kind of distinction typical to Socrates, in this case the difference between doing what one *wants* and doing what *seems best*. Socrates will maintain that both power and wanting must be based on what *is* good and not just what seems good. At the outset, however, it seems to Polus that *being able* to do whatever seems best is "having great power" (466e).

POLUS DOES AGREE quite readily that having great power cannot follow from being able to do whatever seems best if one "doesn't have any sense (*nous*)." Socrates responds by saying,

> Then will you demonstrate that rhetoricians have
> sense and that rhetoric is an art and not pandering by
> refuting me? But if you leave me unrefuted, the rheto-
> ricians who do what seems good to them in their cit-
> ies, and the tyrants as well, will have attained nothing
> good by that. But power is a good thing, as you claim,
> while you also agree that doing what seems good with-
> out sense is a bad thing—don't you? (467a)

Socrates asks Polus to refute him. What does it mean to set refutation as the goal of the conversation? (Note that in asking for refutation, Socrates also makes a point of highlighting aspects of the prior exchanges that Polus has *agreed to*.)

When Socrates presses the difference between *true wants*
and *seeming goods*, Polus accuses Socrates of making "appall-
ing and monstrous statements" (467b). This is one strategy
for refutation—at least as Polus understands refutation. Perhaps, he thinks, he can get Socrates to back down from his
assertions by such an accusation. Socrates resists. Getting
someone to retract a statement is not the same as refuting
what has been said. Socrates asks for Polus to either "display the fact that I'm mistaken" or "answer questions yourself" (467c). Polus again replies admirably: "I'm quite willing to answer questions, so I can know what you're talking
about too."

THESE QUESTIONS lead to the conclusion that a rhetori-
cian or tyrant can "do what seems good to him in a city
without having great power and without doing what he
wants" (468e). Polus acts with good will in his conversa-

tion with Socrates, but he is no sycophant and erupts with incredulity at this point, suggesting that even Socrates himself would readily accept the ability to do whatever seemed good to him and would envy anyone else who could. This eruption shows us something important. The conversations that Socrates engages in are not simply sequences of verbal clarification and logical inference. Polus feels something is amiss in Socrates' line of reasoning and pushes the conversation in the direction of that feeling.

Socrates' response to Polus' eruption of feeling is significant as well. He does not denigrate it as a mere outburst of feeling, but treats it as something worthy of consideration: he asks whether the actions Polus mentioned are done justly or unjustly. Also, by taking up Polus' interjection, Socrates shows himself open to allowing the conversation to be guided by Polus.

SOCRATES GOES ON to explore why the person with free rein is not to be envied if he does not act justly. Polus attempts a second form of refutation. This time he employs a strategy that "even a child could come up with" (470c), namely, pointing to examples that on their face would serve as refutations.

Polus mentions Archelaus, who seized absolute power in Macedonia by means of trickery and force, and the Great King of Persia. If anyone should be envied, surely these men should be since they are undoubtedly happy. That such men are and should be envied seems to be in no need of examination for Polus. *And what is clear without examination even a child can bring forth to refute someone.* In his next long speech, Socrates says that Polus is "trying to refute [him] rhetorically" (471e) by bringing in a parade of witnesses who will assert that he is "not telling the truth" (472a). "But this sort of refutation is worth nothing for getting at truth," Socrates says.

Despite the throngs of people who might indeed speak against Socrates on this matter, he counters with,

> But I, who happen to be one person, do not agree. You can't force me to, although by bringing in many false witnesses against me you're trying to oust me from my birthright, which is the truth. (472b)

It is worth quoting Socrates at length as he continues.

> But if I don't bring you yourself forward as one witness to agree with the things I'm saying, I consider myself as having accomplished nothing worth speaking of in regard to the things our speech may be about. And I consider that you haven't either unless I, only one though I am, am a witness for your side, and you let go of all these others. So there's that one style of refutation, as you and many others imagine, and there's another, which I for my part envision. Now that we've set them alongside one another, let's examine whether there's any difference between them. Because the things about which we're in dispute happen to be no small matters at all, but just about the one it's most beautiful to have knowledge about, and most shameful to lack it, since what they boil down to is recognizing or being ignorant of who's happy and who's not. (472b–d)

A complete picture has emerged of the aim and measure of a conversation for Socrates. It is first of all fundamentally a pursuit for two people. Socrates wants to do something with Polus, here and now. One condition for carrying this out is to set aside the opinions of the many. This means also that common opinions, ones that we ourselves might hold, will be tested. We can bring such opinions into a conversation if things really seem that way to us. That is, common opinions cannot be appealed to just on the basis of being held by many people. And this means that one must really think in such a conversation. Parroting common views will not suffice. Also, we see now that *refutation and agreement go hand in hand.* Socrates and Polus do not agree about certain things that have been said. If they are to come into agreement, then either one of them will have to change his convictions, or both will. But this means that the true measure of the conversation must be those things attested to by the participants themselves. The truth of the matters at hand have to be assessed by means of thoughtful effort by those conversing. Appeals to some other source of authority have to be set aside. The motivation to submit to this way of talking comes from the importance attributed to the things in dispute.

As their conversation continues, seemingly outrageous conclusions are reached, most especially the conclusion that one should strive to ensure that one's family and friends are punished for their unjust acts, but that one should endeavor to have one's enemies go unpunished. Polus' deep discomfort with these conclusions is palpable, and perhaps he is right to be unsettled.

But his response to Socrates toward the end of their conversation is telling. At one point Polus says, "It seems crazy to me, Socrates, but all the same, you know, it agrees with our earlier statements" (480e). This sentiment is precisely what Socrates is trying to engender in Polus—a recognition that, irrespective of where the conversation has arrived, they have arrived there together, that they—the two of them and no one else—have joint ownership of the results of their endeavor.

RECOGNIZING THEIR common ownership of the results of their conversation does not mean Polus and Socrates must now accept these conclusions without further scrutiny. The conditions announced at the beginning of their exchanges can once again be invoked: Anything that has been said can be taken back if further discussion can convince them a mistake was made. (And one kind of mistake is to fail to make all the requisite distinctions in a given case.)

Submitting oneself to the common endeavor of conversation does not entail being slavish toward particular things said in the conversation. And further scrutiny will be needed on those occasions when it is difficult to speak with the forthrightness that is called for. For instance, it is not always possible to distinguish in ourselves genuinely held views from unexamined prejudices. Indeed, it might take a lot of work to expose the latter if our interlocutors hold the same prejudices. Another way in which a conversation can go astray is one we have already encountered, namely withholding one's genuine opinions out of a sense of shame or propriety. It was Polus' contention that Socrates had forced Gorgias to do this. And Callicles will go on to say the same about Polus' agreement that "committing injustice is an uglier thing than suffering it" (482d). It is not clear whether Callicles is correct in what he says about Polus, but the accusation shows us that every conversation is in some respect opaque. Good will and openness do not lead to infallibility.

∎

Socrates said that Polus' way of refuting was "worth nothing for getting at truth." We might think by implication that Socrates' way is. This would seem to be at odds with where we just ended up, that the common endeavor of open dialogue does not guarantee true conclusions.

How can Socrates suggest that this way of inquiry is indeed worth something for attaining truth? In fact, what exactly does Socrates mean by truth here? Socrates does not really say anything in his remarks to Polus to help us out.

Does it have anything to do with where we began? Socrates said that philosophers are "lovers of the sight of the truth." This turned out to be a seeing of forms. Is Socrates' way of conversing a way of seeing forms?

We begin exploring this question with *Phaedrus*. The first half of the dialogue culminates with Socrates' so-called palinode, the taking back of a speech in which he criticizes love (*eros*) as a form of sickness. The palinode is an elaborate speech, full of wild mythological imagery, that praises the madness brought on by *eros* as a gift from a god. The speech includes a mythologically-tinged account of what a soul must undergo to become a human soul.

In order for a soul to be able to enter a human body, that soul must have caught sight of the beings which lie "beyond the heavens." In the imagery of the speech, the Olympian gods ride upon the outer sphere of the heavens, carried along by its motion, and gaze upon these beings. Concerning what the souls of the gods experience, Socrates says:

> Of that place beyond the heavens none of this world's poets has yet sung worthily, nor shall any ever do so.

But it is like this—for one must dare to speak the truth, and especially when the subject is the truth itself. That place is occupied by the being that really is [*ousia ontos ousa*], which is intangible and without color or shape. It is perceived only by the intellect, the pilot of the soul, and is the object of the true kind of knowledge. The mind of a god, which draws its nourishment from intelligence and pure knowledge, and that of every soul that cares about getting what is proper for it, cherishes the opportunity to observe what is and is nourished and happy while it studies the truth during the time it takes the circular revolution to carry it back to its starting point. On its circular journey, it sees justice itself, it sees judiciousness, and it sees knowledge, not the knowledge that is connected with becoming and varies with the varying things we now say are, but rather the knowledge that exists in the realm of what really is and really is knowledge. (247c–e)

Other non-divine souls, pictured as a charioteer pulled by two horses (one tame, the other unruly), must struggle to get above the rim of the heavens to catch a glimpse of what lies out there. This is accomplished only with difficulty and fleetingly. The soul is motivated by the great delight and nourishment offered by gazing upon the beings beyond the heavens. Eventually however, if a soul is unable to be adequately nourished by these visions, it will become "burdened with forgetfulness" (248c), lose its wings, and fall to earth.

WHEN LATER WE LEARN that only a soul which has previously managed some sightings of the beings beyond the heavens can become the soul of a human being, Socrates says:

> A soul that has never seen the truth cannot take on [human] shape, because a human being must under-stand speech [what is said, *legomenon*] according to forms [*kat' eidos*], drawing together [*sunairoumenon*] through reason [reckoning, *logismos*] a one out of many perceptions. (249b–c)

With this passage we see that recourse to forms is not for philosophers only. The back story about how human souls acquire vision of the forms may be mythological, but the assertion concerning their place in all human lives seems straightforward: without recourse to forms, human beings cannot understand speech or grasp "ones" from out of the multiplicity of sense perception. The suggestion, it seems, is that speech would be mere noise without forms and sense perception would be without any nodes of unity and order. In short, no mindful, coherent being-in-the-world would be possible, including that mode of being-in-the-world of such importance to Socrates: conversation. According to the mythological account, all human beings were once like Socrates' philosophers—souls that take delight in a vision of forms. In a moment we will see more about how this prior acquaintance with the forms makes ordinary think-ing and speaking possible. The larger question going for-ward is whether the account of seeing forms can be brought down to earth.

SOCRATES AND PHAEDRUS never really talk in detail about the elaborate images of Socrates' palinode. The con-versation is quickly diverted to questions about what is entailed in giving a good speech. At one point, however,

Socrates seems to gesture back to the passage we just looked at. He says that while his earlier speech was both "playful" and a "mythical hymn" it seems that "among those remarks two principles were mentioned by chance, and if someone could grasp their essence in an artful manner, it wouldn't be insignificant" (256c–d).

These principles concern collecting and dividing and are grounded in one source—the forms. Of collecting, Socrates says it is "bring[ing] together things that are scattered about and see[ing] them in terms of a single form" (256d). Of dividing, Socrates says it is "being able to dissect a thing in accordance with its forms, following the natural joints and not trying to hack it apart like an incompetent butcher" (265e).

Consider someone who is charged with conferring praise on members of some group of people, for example, for displaying a particular virtue. The person conferring praise will strive to gather together the praise-worthy persons, discerning in the actions of each the "same form." But the very discernment that would make this collecting possible is also a dividing, whereby the praise-worthy are separated from those not deserving of praise. Such things are done all the time without any explicit reflection on the fact that collecting and dividing is happening, nor on what makes such collecting and dividing possible.

SOCRATES GOES ON to say,

> I, myself, Phaedrus, am a lover of these dividings and collectings as what enable me to speak and to think, and when I believe that someone else is able to see the natural unity and plurality of things, I follow him. (266b)

The difference between Socrates and others would not be whether they engage in collecting and dividing, but rather in taking delight in these. We might say that Socrates delights not just in the doing but also in being aware that he is doing it. He turns back toward his own speaking and thinking and sees them as collection and division. This in itself is not a seeing of forms. But since Socrates maintains that speech and thought rely on forms, paying attention to speaking and thinking is perhaps a way to catch sight of one.

We turn to *Theaetetus* for some clues about how this might come about.

■

The main thread of discussion in Plato's *Theaetetus* is initiated by Theaetetus' suggestion that knowledge is perception. This answer is given after Socrates presses Theaetetus to give a definition of knowledge that would capture it *under one form*. The suggestion that knowledge is perception is followed by a lengthy investigation of the Protagorean maxim, "Man is the measure of all things," and the notion that the world is entirely in flux.

Much of the discussion about the Protagorean maxim and that "all is flux" occurs not between Socrates and the youthful Theaetetus, but between Socrates and Theodorus, Theaetetus' teacher in mathematics. When that inquiry is brought to an end, Socrates turns to Theaetetus and pursues again, from the beginning as it were, the suggestion that knowledge is perception. This phase of their conversation runs through a number of quick conclusions. The first is that each of the things we call "sensible" relies on a special organ (eyes for color, ears for sounds, etc.) and that these organs are not properly the things with which we see or hear or otherwise sense, but rather those through which we sense. This assertion seems to be based on the fact that our sense experience exhibits unity. The various senses somehow come together in one experience. Socrates and Theaetetus agree that it would not be a bad answer to say that this unity happens by means of the soul. Nevertheless, the various sensibles can ultimately be traced back, in their manyness, to the body (see 184b–e).

Theaetetus also agrees with Socrates that what is perceived by one power (say, color by sight) cannot be perceived by another power (say, hearing). By what organ, then, Socrates wants to know, can we perceive that both sound and color *are*; that they are *different* than each other but the *same* as themselves; that they are together *two*, but each *one*? By what organ will we be able to consider whether they are *alike* or *unlike*, as we can say whether two things are both salty or not by means of the tongue? Theaetetus, clearly a philosophically-minded fellow, gives a good summary of the kinds of things Socrates is asking about: being and not-being, likeness and unlikeness, same and other, one and numbers (see 185a–d).

Theaetetus answers Socrates' question with:

> Well by Zeus, Socrates, I at least would have no way to say, except that it seems to me there's absolutely no such special organ for these things as there is for those others, but the soul itself, through itself, appears to me to observe the common things involved in all things. (185d)

For the sensible things, the bodily organs are the things through which what is perceived is brought to the soul. For these other things, common to the different sensibles, the soul itself is that through which they are brought to the soul. What can this mean?

At first glance it seems that it might just be an infelicitous turn of phrase. Maybe Theaetetus should have said that there is nothing through which the soul acquires a sense of being, or likeness, or number. Maybe it would be best to just say that they are "in" the soul. No "through which" would be required. But if we assume that Theaetetus knows what he means, then we cannot dismiss his phrasing so quickly. (Note as well that this phrasing is in line with the mythological picture offered in *Phaedrus*. There the forms come into the soul through the soul itself when they are glimpsed above the heavens and are recollected in human life through memory.)

Socrates is pleased by Theaetetus' answer, saying that it is beautiful and that Theaetetus spared him "a very long speech." Socrates makes clear at this point that he and Theaetetus have set up two classes of things, those that come to the soul through the body, on the one hand, and those that come to the soul through itself on the other. He asks Theaetetus to which *being* belongs. "I place it among the things the soul itself, by itself, reaches out for [*eporegetai*, aims at, desires]" (186a). This answer again repeats an element of the *Phaedrus* account, that contact with the forms is motivated by desire. I think all we can note at this point from Theaetetus' perspective is that the "through itself" of the soul cannot be construed as passive reception. To the extent that being comes through the soul it is as a result of *desirous reaching out*.

IT SEEMS THAT we have not come very far if Theaetetus is just repeating in his own way what we already saw in Socrates' *Phaedrus* speech. The next stretch of the conversation will help us make an advance.

When Socrates goes on to ask whether the soul also reaches out for the like and the unlike, for the same and other, for beautiful and ugly, and for good and bad, Theaetetus answers:

> It seems to me that it's the being of these as well that [the soul] looks to, especially in their relations to one another, gathering up [*analogizomai*, reckon up, calculate] in itself the past and present things in relation to the future ones. (186a)[6]

Theaetetus suggests that the soul "looks to" these things, in its reaching out, by a gathering up, a reckoning, or calculating. Initially, we should simply note that the soul is doing something. What it is doing might best be approached by breaking down the Greek word. *Analogizomai* is made up of the prefix *ana-*, suggesting an up and down movement, and *logizomai*, indicating a kind of calculative thinking. (Let us also note that *logizomai* can be traced back to *logos*, speech, reason.) It seems then that when the soul looks to those things that come to it through the soul, it does so by engaging in a calculating that moves up and down between things, keeping an eye on their relations to one another.

SOCRATES SEEMS to endorse Theaetetus' suggestion in a series of remarks. In the first he says that the soul works at discriminating (*krino*) the things that come to the soul through itself by "going back over (*epaneimi*) them" and "comparing (*sumballo*) them to one another" (186b). In a question that follows, Socrates suggests that what does not come through the body is gathered up (*analogizomai*) only "with difficulty and over time, through many troubles and through education" (186c). After then suggesting that truth, and hence knowledge, can be reached only through reaching for being, Socrates says:

> Therefore, knowledge is not present in the experiences, but in the process of gathering together [*sullogismos*] what's involved in them, for in the latter, as it seems, there is power to come in touch with being and truth . . . (186d)

Knowledge, inasmuch as it depends on those things that come to the soul through itself, cannot be obtained simply by having experiences. One must work on them. That work, it seems, is most especially a kind of thinking that reckons through gathering.

We will do well to note that the words analogy and syllogism come directly from or are related to *analogizomai* and *sullogismos*. The kind of work that Theaetetus and Socrates seem to have in mind, as related to analogy and syllogisms, entails finding correspondences in relations between otherwise disparate things, on the one hand, and drawing conclusions by assembling statements as premises in a line of reasoning, on the other. With this we have come around in a circle. In the passages from the second half of *Phaedrus* that we looked at, Socrates suggested that collecting and dividing guided by forms enabled him to speak and think. The passages from *Theaetetus* just considered suggest that forms (i.e., those things that come to the soul through itself) are gotten at by means of speaking and thinking.

Can we have it both ways?

ANOTHER PASSAGE from *Theaetetus* may help show that ordinary conversation does indeed entail both of these aspects. The passage will not reveal how conversation can bring about a vision of a form "itself by itself." But it may help us understand how there can be a connection between *relying on* forms and *searching for* a form.

Much of the *Theaetetus* is concerned with questioning the coherence of Protagoras' maxim that "Man is the measure of all things." This comes about because Socrates suggests this maxim is equivalent to the claim that knowing is perceiving. He also suggests that the maxim is equivalent to the assertion that the world is a realm of total flux. How all of these connections are made is worthy of study, but we make note of them here only to provide some context for the passage quoted below.

The passage concerns motion, which Socrates and Theodorus agree must be considered if the coherence of the notion that all is flux is to be assessed. Socrates and Theodorus have the following set of exchanges:

SOC: It seems to me, then, that the starting point [*arche*] for an examination about motion is: what sort of thing are they talking about when they say that all things are in motion? I mean to say something like this: are they talking about some one form [*eidos*] of it, or, as it appears to me, two? However, don't let it seem that way only to me, but you too take share in it with me, so that we'll undergo in common anything there's a need for. And tell me, do you call it moving whenever something changes from place to place or even turns around in the same place?

THEO: I do.

SOC: Then let this be one form. But whenever something is in the same place, but gets old, or becomes black from white or hard from soft, or alters by any other sort of alteration, isn't it worth declaring that a different form of motion?

THEO: It's necessary, in fact.

SOC: Then by two forms of motion I'm speaking of this pair, alteration and change of place.

THEO: And speaking correctly.

SOC: Accordingly, now that we've divided this in that way, let's now have a discussion with those who claim all things are in motion, and ask: do you claim that everything is in motion in both ways, being carried around and altering, or one thing in both ways and another thing in one of the two? (181c–e)

Socrates and Theodorus are trying to get a handle on what motion is. Although they do not cast it this way, we might say that they are trying to get a glimpse of the "look" of motion, to see motion "itself by itself."

Socrates asks if change of place is a kind—form—of motion. Theodorus agrees that it is. In doing so, Theodorus implicitly assents to being able to recognize many and various changes as being of one kind. We might say that these changes "look" the same to him. He is even ready to include spinning motions within this look. Furthermore, he is comfortable referring to this gathering of many changes into one kind with the designation of *eidos*. Being able to collect according to a form and understand what is said in terms of that form does not, however, it seems, need to entail being "able to catch sight of" the form itself. In this respect, the remarks above only illustrate the picture we have laid out already.

That picture is repeated when Socrates asks about the second kind of motion. Again, Theodorus recognizes right away that the examples Socrates offers fall into one kind. He is even ready at once to assign the name "alteration" to this kind. So here we have another example of what Socrates meant when he said that collecting and dividing by means of form are what "enable [him] to speak and to think."

The other element of this passage that we need to take note of is that the delineation of these two kinds is in the service of getting a better view of the one kind that is motion itself. In zeroing in successively on change of place and alteration, as forms for collecting certain motions, motion is divided by means of kind. But this dividing does not leave us with a heterogeneous two. Change of place and alteration are not kinds that are indifferent to one another. They go together since they are both kinds within one kind. Pausing to discriminate change of place and alteration turns out to be a step in attempting to get a clearer look at motion in general.

Our small example here seems also to illustrate what Theaetetus and Socrates discussed. By first going back and forth between changes of place and spinnings, and then between changes of color, hardness, and other qualities, two forms of motion were clarified. It seems that the next step would be to then go back and forth between these kinds themselves to get clarity on the greater kind, motion as such.

■

If this speech about motions shows better how forms are at work in the search through speech for a form, it does not show us what it looks like to find a form, to catch sight of it itself by itself. Is there a way, finally, to see someone discern one form in speech? Another section of *Theaetetus* will get us closer. Theaetetus himself provides an example through a discussion of a problem in geometry.

This discussion occurs near the beginning of the dialogue. Shortly after being introduced to Theaetetus, Socrates engages him in an investigation concerning the nature of knowledge, about what it means to know something. Socrates presses him to state the one thing that knowledge is. This is what Theaetetus says:

> It seems to me, then, both that the things one might learn from Theodorus are pieces of knowledge, geometry and what you went over just now, and also skill at leather-cutting and the arts of the other craftsmen— each and every one of these is nothing other than knowledge. (146c–d)

Socrates replies,

> It's certainly well bred and generous of you, dear fellow, when you're asked for one thing, to give many and varied things instead of something simple. (146d)

That is, as Socrates goes on to explain, he did not ask for instances of knowledge, or those things of which there is knowledge, but for what knowledge itself is. Socrates is looking for the one thing that knowledge is rather than the many ways that knowledge can be obtained.

THEAETETUS QUICKLY grasps why Socrates is dissatisfied with his answer and thinks he has just been through a different investigation that did arrive at the kind of thing Socrates is looking for. Theaetetus walks Socrates through this other matter before proposing that the one thing that knowledge is is perception.

This other investigation that Theaetetus describes concerns the problem of how to classify the lengths of the sides of squares. The problem can be laid out as follows, even if some of the terms would be foreign to Theaetetus.

Imagine an array of squares, the areas of which correspond to whole numbers. The first (unit) square would have both an area of one square unit and sides of one unit of length. A square of four square units could easily be obtained by assembling four of these unit squares into a larger square. It is readily evident that the square with an area of four square units has sides of two units of length. This already gives us part of Theaetetus' approach to the problem, as we will see below.

But we skipped over the squares with areas of two and three square units. What are the lengths of their sides?[7] It is easy to see that their lengths cannot correspond to whole numbers. A length of one linear unit yields a square with an area of one; a length of two linear units yields a square with an area of four. The sides of squares with areas of two and three square units must be greater than one unit of length and less than two. But how much greater or less?

Answering this opens up one of the great discoveries of Greek mathematics and is the key to Theaetetus' solution to the problem. The discovery is that of incommensurable lengths. What does incommensurable mean here? One might think that a common unit of measurement can be found for any two lines, say, the side of a square and its diagonal. The side itself cannot be the measure, since one side length falls short of the diagonal and two exceed it. But maybe some proper part of the side length will work, say, the half, or the third, or the fourth. That is, it looks as if it might be the case that if one split the length of the side into some number of parts of equal length (it could be a hundred, or a million), that one of those parts could be used to measure exactly the length of the diagonal.

It can be proven that this is not the case. The side and diagonal of a square have no common measure of length.[8] One way to express this is that there is no way to *say* how long the diagonal of a square is if we use a length that measures exactly a side of that square. Lines such as the side and diagonal of a square are said by Euclid to be *alogon*, usually translated as irrational, but which could be construed as un-sayable.

But it is easy to say this: The square built on the diagonal has twice the area of the square of which it is the diagonal. (If this is not evident to you, take a minute to persuade yourself that it is so.) So while the length of the diagonal is un-sayable as measured by the side, the ratio of the lines is sayable "in square." That is, there is something quite definite (and simple) in the relation between these two lengths, but that definite relation has to do with the areas of the squares built on them and not on their lengths.

WE NOTED ABOVE that the square with an area of four and side of two was easily obtained by building a new square using four unit squares. Notice that squares with areas of nine, sixteen, twenty-five and so on are also easily obtained in the same way. And in each case the side length will be a whole number: three, four, five and so on. We need to note as well that *if* two squares have sides that are commensurable, then those squares have to each other the same ratio as some pair of "square" numbers. Why? If to be commensurable in length means to have a common unit of measurement, then the ratio of the lengths must correspond to the ratio of two whole numbers. Imagine two squares whose sides are measured out exactly by the same unit of length, eleven times in one case and thirteen in the other. (We can imagine a ruler being placed eleven times and thirteen times, respectively, along the sides of these squares.) The squares will contain 121 and 169 unit squares, respectively. Or will have areas of 121 and 169 square units. Or will have areas of 11×11 and 13×13 square units. However we express it, we can see that if commensurability of lines means that the lines have the ratio of a whole number to a whole number, then the squares built on them will always have areas corresponding to square numbers and therefore the ratio of the areas of the squares to each other will be as a ratio of (some pair of) square numbers.

LET US RETURN to *Theaetetus*. When Theaetetus grasps the defect of his first answer about what knowledge is and mentions that the kind of thing that Socrates is looking for may have come up in this other inquiry, he says,

> Theodorus here was diagramming something for us about potencies[9], demonstrating about the potential side of the three-foot square and about that of the five-foot square that they are not commensurable in length with the foot-long line, and demonstrating in this way as he picked out each of them one by one up to the seventeen-foot square; at that one, for some reason, he got tangled up. So something of this sort occurred to us: since the potential squares are obviously infinite in multitude, we would try to gather them together into some one thing, in which we could address our speech to all these potential squares. (147d–e)

The proofs that Theaetetus mentions endeavor to show that the sides of the squares with areas of three, five, and others up to (but not including) seventeen are in fact incommensurable with a unit length. (The square with area of two is not mentioned, I think, because proofs of the incommensurability of its sides with a unit length were probably well known to those involved in the discussion.) While not explicitly mentioned, it seems evident that proofs would not be given for squares with areas of nine and sixteen, since it is easily shown that their sides *are* commensurable. This is already indicated by Theaetetus skipping over the square with an area of four square units. Furthermore, Theaetetus points out that *each new square requires its own proof.* That is, there are many proofs needed to separate the squares with commensurable sides from those with incommensurable ones.

THEAETETUS SHOWS that he is already attuned to Socrates' request for a definition of knowledge in terms of one thing when he remarks that he (seemingly spontaneously) aimed for such a thing in this case. In the case of classifying the sides of squares as commensurable or incommensurable, Theaetetus asked himself: Is there one account that separates all squares with areas of whole numbers into two classes, those with commensurable sides and those without?

It turns out there is since it can be shown that if two squares do not have a ratio that is the same as a ratio of two square numbers, then their sides are not commensurable. As we saw above, if the sides are commensurable, then the squares must have a ratio that is the same as the ratio of some pair of square numbers. Taken together, these statements allow us to divide all squares with areas of whole numbers, at one stroke, into two classes. The sides of squares with areas corresponding to square numbers will be commensurable with the sides of other such squares. The sides of all of the other squares will be incommensurable both with each other and with the sides of the first class.

WE CAN NOW see why Theaetetus "gets" what Socrates is after in his question about knowledge. Socrates does not want a list of examples, or even a proof that geometry *is* knowledge and that the craft of leather-cutting *is* knowledge, and so on. He wants one account that will cover all the instances, just as Theaetetus' account about the sides of squares covers everything with one account.

But we can also see how much work it might take to hit on such an account! Our path through the problem of the squares only indicated the main lines of argument. A fully grounded account would take much longer and would require far more precision. Suffice it to say, coming to possess one account for a multitude of cases is not pictured here as a simple act of seeing (even if cracking the problem comes in a flash of insight).

In fact, what we went through concerning the squares could stand as a strong example of the work of *analogizomai* and *sullogismos* we considered earlier. Theaetetus does not wait around for an answer to simply appear. He sifts through the material, making comparisons and distinctions. He asks what follows from the things he discerns and endeavors to glean "one thing" from out of this sifting and reasoning.

■

It is not immediately clear how to categorize what Theaetetus has accomplished. His account enables us to see at once which squares have commensurable sides and which ones do not. Perhaps we could say that the squares with commensurable sides have a common "look" inasmuch as they have areas that correspond to square numbers. In this way, Theaetetus has enabled us to see through the thicket of particular squares to something not directly visible. In our discussion of *Meno* below, this feature will show its importance, for the look Theaetetus reveals is an *intelligible look*, something only approachable through thinking about the array of squares with areas corresponding to whole numbers. Looking at the squares in the usual sense, even measuring them, will not disclose the way to separate them by kind.

Perhaps we can construe Theaetetus' work as an answer to the question "What is a commensurable side of a square?" It seems more apt, however, to cast Theaetetus' work as an answer to a question about *how* to distinguish one kind of square from another. It has been helpful, though, to see that this how can be considered as springing from the disclosure of the intelligible look of squares whose sides are commensurable.

In what ways, though, might this mathematical question differ from the question that prompted the discussion of squares in the first place, "What is knowledge?" Indeed, what might be unique in general about questions like "What is virtue?," "What is friendship?," or "What is justice?"? Consider first this difference: unlike commensurability, things like knowledge, virtue, friendship, and justice are matters of common concern; furthermore, they are things which everyone, in some sense, already understands.

Notice as well that these "What is . . . ?" questions can be thought of as asking for definitions. Theaetetus' question about the squares was not really a question of definition, and a careful excavation of his solution to the problem of determining which sides of squares are commensurable would show that it relies ultimately on certain clear-cut definitions. Indeed, this would be a decisive difference between mathematical and non-mathematical inquiry: in the one case, definitions are laid down at the beginning; in the other, the search for definitions is the principal pursuit.

If there is common ground between Theaetetus' geometric undertaking and the pursuit of a "What is . . . ?" question, then we want to know what it would mean to achieve for the likes of knowledge, virtue, friendship, and justice what Theaetetus achieved for squares with commensurable sides.

We turn to Plato's *Meno* for a final pass at this question.

THE *MENO* BEGINS abruptly. It is a direct dialogue, so we have no narration of setting or circumstance. The first speech is by Meno, and he asks whether Socrates can tell him how virtue is acquired. Socrates wants to know whether the question can be answered if one does not know what virtue is.[10] Meno thinks not, but is surprised to hear that Socrates might not know what virtue is! The next few exchanges exhibit some of the features of Socratic conversation that we have encountered above. It will be good to take note of them again.

First, Socrates is ready to admit that he does not know what virtue is. We might recall that Polus said Gorgias got into trouble in his conversation with Socrates because he found it shameful to say that he might not know what justice is. One suspects Meno's reaction to Socrates has a bit of this in it. Whether Socrates does in fact not know what virtue is, Meno seems surprised to hear him say it out loud.

Second, we might not be surprised at this since Socrates mentions that Gorgias is Meno's teacher at the beginning of his initial reply. Meno leans on his relationship with Gorgias and ask Socrates, "What? You didn't happen to meet Gorgias when he was here?" "I did," Socrates replies. Meno then asks, "Really—did he not seem to you to know?" (71c). It seems that Meno's question can be taken at least two ways. On the one hand, he might really trust in Gorgias' wisdom and think that what Gorgias says about virtue is correct. On the other hand, he might think that even if Gorgias does not really know what virtue is, he has *said* what it is, and one can hide one's own ignorance by repeating what someone else has said. A third possibility is that Meno does not really distinguish between these two— talking persuasively and knowing might look the same to him. However one comes down on this, Socrates makes it moot by asking that he and Meno set aside what others have said about virtue and that the two of them take up the investigation together. We see Socrates setting the stage to attempt what he undertook with Polus.

THE NEXT SET of exchanges repeats something we saw between Socrates and Theaetetus. Meno ventures a definition of virtue, but begins by making a list, stating first what virtue is for a man and then for a woman. He continues,

> And the virtue of child is different, both female and male, and of an elderly man, and, if you want, of a freeman or, if you want, of a slave. And there are a great many other virtues, so that there is no difficulty in speaking about what virtue is. For according to each activity and each time of life relative to each task for each of us there is a virtue, and in the same way, I suppose, Socrates, there is also vice. (71e–72a)

Socrates responds with a wonderful image. While asking for the one thing that virtue is, he says that Meno has

given him a *swarm*. One can imagine the many virtues
Meno has mentioned buzzing around Socrates' head. The
swarm makes it easy to talk about virtue. This is because
it is just easier to talk about what is good for a particular type of person to do, or what is good to do in certain
kinds of activities, than it is to give a general definition. We
might compare this with Theaetetus' discourse about the
sides of squares. At first it seemed easier to take the squares
one at a time and provide a separate proof for each. But this
approach comes to look foolhardy once the general account
is hit upon. Socrates is going to press Meno for something
like the solution to the mathematical problem. Is it possible in this case? If not, is there nevertheless something to be
gained from the attempt?

THE NEXT SET of remarks needs closer attention.

> SOC: [. . .] But, Meno, following up this image about
> swarms, if after you have been asked by me about the
> very being of a bee, just what it is, and you were say-
> ing that there are many and all sorts, what would you
> answer me if I asked you: "Then are you saying that
> they are many and of all sorts and different from one
> another in this by which they are bees? Or that it is not
> this in which they differ, but in something else, such as
> beauty or size or something else of this sort?" Tell me,
> what would you answer after being questioned in this
> way?

> MENO: I would answer this, that they do not differ,
> one from the other, in that by which they are bees.

> SOC: If then I were to say after that: "Tell me further,
> Meno, this very thing in which they do not differ but

are all the same thing, what do you say that is?" You
could, I suppose, tell me what it is?

MENO: I could.

SOC: And so too, surely, about the virtues: even if
they are many and of all sorts, still they all have some
one and the same form [*eidos*] through which they are
virtues and upon which one would somehow do well
to focus one's gaze, that is, the one answering him
who has asked him to clarify that, namely, what does
virtue happen to be. Or do you not understand what
I'm saying?

MENO: It seems to me that I do understand. Yet
somehow I don't grasp what is being asked as well as I
would like. (72a–d)

Socrates' question about bees shows that difference does
not need to exclude sameness. Bees can differ without differing inasmuch as they are bees. Indeed, this seems, again,
to be built in to the way we talk. If we mean something
that is the same when we use the word "bee," but do not
intend our meaning to deny any differences between the
things marked out by the word, then in one respect Socrates' question need not go beyond what is intended in ordinary speech. In another respect, his way of putting the matter might go beyond what is intended in ordinary speech
by asking about "that by which" bees are bees. This seems
to tip into metaphysical questions about the ground of the
sameness of bees as a kind of being.

Meno does not hesitate about this phrasing and agrees
that bees cannot differ "in that by which they are bees."
His ready agreement, I think, could spring simply from

the ordinariness of what is being asked about. Bees are bees after all. His answer to the next question, however, is puzzling. Socrates suggests that it would be easy for Meno to say what this thing is by which bees are bees, and Meno agrees. He says he could tell Socrates what this is. I can only think that Meno is either lying or not thinking or doesn't really understand how tricky the question is. Perhaps a close associate of Socrates would have an answer ready: "That by which bees are bees is the form of bee." But what does that mean? We have seen previously that forms are appealed to as what make speech and thought possible; that a certain kind of searching in speech and thought reaches out to forms; and that positing form-like definitions is put forward as a way of initiating a conversation. But we have not seen an account of what a form is or how it can be the thing that makes many things the same in some way.

SOCRATES HIMSELF glosses over such questions when he uses the language of forms in his next speech. While he leaves behind mentioning bees, we might paraphrase his remarks as saying that just as there is one form through which bees are bees, so must there be one form through which virtues are virtues. Much of what we have been through in this chapter seems condensed in what Socrates says next, that "one would somehow do well to focus one's gaze [upon the form]." Here again we see that Socrates is not so much concerned with questions about what a form is or how they make contact with many things, but instead with appealing to forms as a way of *gathering our attention*. It seems *good for us* to speak and think in this way.

There is a simple difference of major consequence, however, between bees and virtues, namely, that one set of things is visible and the other is not. I think it is easy for Meno to assent that there is some one thing that bees have in common since they all look like bees. But what does it mean to say that all virtues look like virtues, or that the virtues have a look?—for the virtues are not visible.

The attitude that Socrates calls for, it seems, must fall somewhere between Meno and Theaetetus. I take it that Meno's subsequent admission of confusion likely springs from this move from the visible to invisible. He is not philosophical because he lacks experience of the invisible looks of things. Theaetetus understands what it means to discern something in thought. All of his squares look the same to the eye; but his nuanced account concerning square numbers and incommensurability divides those visibly similar figures into two distinct intelligible classes. But by relying on a geometrical example, it seems that Theaetetus might not be able see the deep puzzles and wonder which an eye for invisible looks can bring about. For all of the power and decisiveness of Theaetetus' solution to the problem concerning squares, his way of setting out lacks the aiming at an intelligible look that Socrates seems to foreground. By both asking "What is . . . ?" and insisting on an answer that has the unity of Theaetetus' solution, Socrates' way of setting out clears a space to see a form—if it is there!

For one making the effort Socrates is endorsing, the turning toward forms is simultaneously grounding and unsettling. Striving to glimpse a form by means of inquiry with others brings focus to our pursuits. But with an eye for forms come all the questions we have set aside concerning how exactly forms could be the principles at work in the sensible world. The focus made possible by searching for forms is also a provocation.

■

The passages from the *Republic* with which we began sketched a picture of the philosopher as the one who is awake and whose wakefulness springs from his delighted vision of the forms among sensible things. And hence being awake would also mean having true knowledge of genuine beings. In *Gorgias* we see Socrates talking something through with Polus, but it seems to be a conversation that begins and ends in opinion. Socrates wants to encourage Polus to strive to bring forth his opinions with clarity and to think them through with rigor. Using the picture in the *Republic* as a measure, one would have to say that Socrates' conversation with Polus is not philosophical since it is not premised on apprehension of forms. The other passages we have looked at suggest, however, that Socrates and his interlocutors occupy a position *between* the picture of the philosopher as the one with clear sight of the forms and someone totally absorbed in opinion. Delight taken in collecting and dividing; reaching out in searching speech to things that come to the soul through itself; setting up a conversation with an attempt to catch an invisible look: all of these are, as it were, a leaning toward knowing, or an incipient movement away from opinion and the opinable to knowledge and being. It is like the brief moment when one is roused from the daydream, still somewhat absorbed by it, but feeling pulled toward something else. In that moment, we begin to see the dream as a dream. Perhaps Socrates' definition of the philosopher is itself only an ideal. Perhaps philosophy as encouraged by Socrates is not being awake, but only an effort to wake up. Perhaps true philosophy happens in this effort.

WORLD

To ask how to begin.

WE FIND OURSELVES speaking. We find ourselves both striving and expecting to be understood. We find ourselves intending to mean something when we speak. Aristotle suggests that our aiming at meaning is built into speech. He captures this thought (in the third book of his *Metaphysics*) in terms of the so-called principle of contradiction.

The principle itself reads: "It is not possible for the same thing at the same time both to belong and not belong to the same thing in the same respect" (1005b19–21). *It is not possible for it to be raining right here, right now and for it not to be raining right here, right now. It is not possible for this table to be made of wood and also not made of wood. It is not possible for Socrates to be seated and not seated. It is not possible for Socrates to be a human being and not be a human being.* Aristotle makes clear that certain qualifications might need to be made in order to see the force of the principle in a given case. One might object to the first example by saying, "It's raining on the east side of town but not on the west." But that must mean that we didn't mean the whole town by "right here." What if the table is held together with nails? Doesn't that mean that it both is and is not made of wood (at the same time)? Sure, but not in the same respect. The table is made of wood in just the way that it is made of wood. The presence of the nails does nothing to alter that. Whatever ambiguities might be involved in someone being seated, if it is true in some respect that Socrates is seated, then he cannot not be seated in that way (just now). Is there any way in which Socrates could be a human being while also not being one?

Shortly after introducing the principle, Aristotle refers to it as an "ultimate opinion" (1005b33). This opinion—this way in which things seem to be—stands behind and supports all of our assertions. This is its ultimacy. If I mean to say that Socrates really is seated (in some specified way), then I must already be of the opinion that he cannot be regarded as *not* seated, just now, in that way. If I were not of this opinion, then what would be the point of making the assertion? If I were of the opinion that it is equally possible that Socrates is not seated here and now, what could I mean by saying that he is? I might indeed make some sounds in uttering the words, but can I be making an attempt at meaning something?

Aristotle approaches this question by considering someone who denies the principle. He says there are such people and that they "themselves claim that it is possible for the same thing to be and not be, and also claim that it is possible to conceive something this way" (1006a1–3). It seems that such a claim is not so much false as that it is nonsense. What does this mean? Certain statements can be false while making perfect sense if they could be true. It might be false that it is raining just now, but the claim that it is raining now could be true if indeed it were raining. The at-this-time-false statement "It is raining" makes sense. A denial of the principle of contradiction, on the other hand, might be grammatically well-formed, but has no sense. It is akin to a phrase like "square circle," which is formed of perfectly intelligible English words, but taken together have no meaning at all.

Does "be" mean something different from "not be"? If not, what follows? Aristotle asks us to entertain the thought that the words "human being" point to one particular meaning, "two-footed animal."[1] He continues, "Now by signifying one thing, I mean this: if this [i.e., being a two-footed animal] is a human being, then if anything is a human being, this will be its being-human" (1006a32–33). I want to mean something when I say "human being." I commit myself, when using the words "human being," to having them point to a certain meaning: two-footed animal. When I say "human being" I mean also "two-footed animal" since I have already asserted that to *be* a human being is to be a two-footed animal. "Two-footed animal" then is not just a substitution for the words "human being," but is intended to capture the *being-human* of the human being. Hence Aristotle: "Now it is not possible that being-human should mean just exactly *not* being-human, if 'human being' not only signifies something belonging to one thing but also one meaning" (1006b13–15).

We started with the question of meaningful speech. Why then this talk of being and not being? As Aristotle's discussion unfolds the connection is brought out ever more fully. Aristotle makes it clear that what he is talking about is not just the stipulated meaning of words. Aristotle is perfectly aware that one person could mean when uttering "human being" what someone else means when uttering "not human being." "But the thing raising an impasse," Aristotle goes on to say, "is not this, whether it is possible for the same thing at the same time to be and not be a human being *in name*, but in respect to *the thing*" (1006b21–22). The meaning of meaningful speech is rooted not in words but in things. To say that "human being" means "two-footed animal" is to say that a certain (kind of) thing is (essentially) a certain way. The thing *is* that way. My speech points to a way of being. I mean it to point in this way.

Thus when Aristotle goes on to consider the implications that would follow if "human being" and "not human being" did not mean anything different, it is not verbal meaning that he is concerned with. His question is about what follows if there is no difference between being human and not being human. We can see fairly readily two complementary implications. First, if the difference between being and not being a human being is no difference, then we cannot hold to the assertion that being a two-footed animal is the being-human of a human being. Or we could if we also allowed "two-footed animal" to mean "not being a human being." But can we allow this? Will words have any meaning if such concessions are made? Maybe, but with this consequence: all words will mean everything; all words will be the same. Secondly, nothing will be anything if being and not being are the same. Nothing will be anything in particular. Nothing will be this *and not* that. But this means that being will lack all determination. There will be nothing about which to say anything. Once again, meaningful speech and the difference between being and not being stand and fall together.

SOMEONE IS ASKED a simple question (for example, "Is this a human being?") and refuses to give a simple answer. The answer instead comes in the form of "Yes, but . . ."

"Yes, this is a human being, but it is also tall and edu-cated." Aristotle seems to think that such an answer har-bors the conviction that the thing in question both is and is not a human being. Someone who answers all questions in this way sees the world in such a way that everything would seem both to be and not be. (We might note in pass-ing that Aristotle points out at the end of the chapter that even people who talk this way do not act accordingly. Aris-totle remarks that when someone has in mind to meet, say, a friend, that person does not go looking for just anything, or for what is not a human being. Setting out to seek this friend in a crowd implies that there is something definite that he is undertaking.)

If one wants to answer simple questions in this way one should do so thoroughly. Why stop when pointing out that the thing that is a human being is also not one because it is tall and educated? There will be other predicates that can be said of the thing. If one mentions that the thing is tall and educated out of scrupulousness, should one not com-plete the list of ways in which the thing is not a human being? Can such a list be completed? Aristotle says such a list would be infinite. If this is the case, and one were to fol-low through on this scrupulousness, Aristotle says conver-sation would not be possible. Every assertion would have to be followed by an endless string of denials. Dialogue would be replaced by a stupid monologue.

BUT IS THE REQUEST for a simple answer—and the possi-bility of conversation—an act of unscrupulousness? Is Aris-totle suggesting that we ignore the (infinitely) long answer so that we can talk to each other, even though this would mean leaving things out? That is, is he suggesting that con-versation entails a noble lie? Are we to think that real talk would require each speaker to go on endlessly in order to state thoroughly any state of affairs, but since that is not feasible, we will agree to settle for simple answers?

In light of what was said above, we can indeed give simple answers because simple determinate things are the case. Or, more carefully stated, our intentions to speak meaningfully entail the assumption of determinateness already. This is not to deny that simplicity is always accompanied by complexity. To take up an example from above, consider the wooden table held together with nails. To the question, "Is this table in some respect made of wood?," a simple "Yes" can be given. It can be given because the simple answer does not ignore the presence of the nails. It also does not ignore the shape of the table, or its height, or its location. The question itself picked out something from this complexity and asked about only that. A "Yes, but . . ." answer is not a better answer to the question asked, since it does not answer the question in a form that is appropriate. Such an answer reveals poor judgment, not scrupulousness.

It turns out, however, that the simple question we borrowed from Aristotle above—"Is this a human being?"—is a loaded question, for lurking in the question is another question. If it turns out to be true that this thing that is a human being is also tall and educated, are all of those ways of being on equal footing? Are the statements "That thing is a human being" and "That thing is tall" the same kind of statement? Grammatically they are the same. But is it possible that we mean something different by the two statements? We will have to delay taking up these questions, but can sketch a hypothetical implication. If being-human is a mode of essential and not incidental being, then the question "Is that thing a human being?" is not the same kind of question as "Is that thing tall." It would be the kind of question to which a simple and unqualified answer can be given most of all. "Is that a human being?" "*Yes.*" Full stop.

IF THE CONSIDERATIONS sketched above are sound, the implications are that the ordinary act of trying to mean something when speaking is rooted in a hidden, prior conviction; that this conviction standing at the base of meaningful speech is at the same time a conviction about beings; and that meaningful speech and determinate being stand together. The ultimacy and priority of the principle of contradiction prevent it from being proven deductively. Its application is already assumed in any proof. But this means that there is no proof that speech can be meaningful and that being is determinate. Rather, tracing the contours of the principle and its implications reveals what is already the case for us who strive to speak meaningfully—that there is a world, and that we are in it. Aristotle begins precisely here—in the world.

■

What is a world? From above, we might begin by saying that a world features determinate things—things about which it is the case that some things can be said and others not. (That is, a world entails the principle of contradiction!) If something common can be said of many things, those things can be separated from the other many things and gathered together. Determining what can be said of things allows for separation and collection. Such separation and collection places things into groupings by kind. For example, one could group objects by color, or size, or shape. One could group people by age or place of birth. The possibilities of grouping are as vast as what can be said of things. But are some groupings more apt than others? Are some of what is said of things more fundamental than others? Are there ways of carving up the world that get at its modes of determination better than others?

Aristotle begins the second book of his *Physics* by delineating two groups: "Of the things that are, some are by nature, others through other causes" (192b8–9). We will come to see that the discernment of this difference is another starting point for Aristotle's thinking. He tells us right away which kinds of things are by nature: "animals and their parts, plants, and the simple bodies such as earth, fire, air and water."[2] This is followed by the assertion that things that are by nature "obviously differ from the things not put together by nature."[3] The crux of the matter for our consideration of Aristotle's ways of beginning is the "obviously" in this statement. On what basis can Aristotle lean on obviousness in a philosophical work? We will have to wade further into the text to answer this question.

EACH THING that is by nature "has in itself a source of motion and rest, either in place, or by growth and shrinkage, or by alteration" (192b12–14). An oak tree produces acorns. One of these acorns finds purchase in the soil and sprouts. Over the years, the sprout increases in size and changes in appearance. Some decades later, this tree comes to resemble the one its seed came from and begins to form acorns itself. A female sparrow lays a fertilized egg. An embryo develops within the egg through growth and alteration. The baby bird breaks out of the egg and continues to grow in size and change in appearance. Eventually the young bird comes to resemble its mother in look and behavior and leaves the nest. Such things seem to happen from themselves. Given the right conditions, the acorn will germinate and develop into an oak tree. It does not seem to need guidance from without. The baby bird may rely on its mother for nourishment, but the unfolding of its bodily development and its inclination to behave in certain ways seem to come from within.

"But a bed or a cloak . . . to the extent that it is from art, has no innate impulse to change at all" (192b14–20). When a carpenter puts together wood, glue, and nails to make a bed, the principle of change is not in the bed. When wool is spun into thread, woven and made into a cloak, the principle of change is not in the cloak. I will call our attention only to Aristotle's suggestion that *obviously* there is difference between oak trees and sparrows on the one hand, and beds and cloaks on the other. Obviously, with oak trees and sparrows no art is required in the formation of the tree and bird, but it is needed to make beds and cloaks.[4] It seems to me that to defend the obviousness of the matter, Aristotle might simply ask us to look on as the acorn grows into the tree and the wood, glue, and nails become a bed. Indeed, the Greek word translated as "obviously" is *phainetai*, related to words for light and visibility, and meaning more literally "to come to light, be seen." Does not the building of a bed look different from the growing of a tree?

HERE'S A POSSIBLE sophisticated answer to the last question: The growing of the tree and the building of the bed may look different to the naïve observer, but underneath they are the same. They are the same because they are part of nature—nature conceived as consisting of some fundamental stuff (matter, forces, energy, etc.) and laws that the stuff obeys. Everything is constituted by the same stuff and the stuff is constrained to behave according to certain laws.

One particularly elegant version of this picture of nature can be found in Descartes' *Le Monde*.[5] In what he calls a "fable," Descartes sketches a streamlined vision of nature. In this fable, God creates a universe filled with matter—matter which can be exhaustively described in terms of size, shape, speed, and position. Once God has set these pieces of matter in motion, his role is to preserve the laws that govern the resulting collisions—laws which, in part, conserve the total quantity of motion in the universe.[6]

Much could be said about Descartes' fable, but I want to highlight two aspects of this picture of the world. The first is that in such a picture, nature is understood to consist in both the moving matter and the laws which such motions obey.[7] Having this in mind will help us see an important difference in Aristotle's conception of nature. The second point concerns rest. In Descartes' picture there is no true rest. This can be seen in two ways. First, if the world is only matter in motion, then motion and rest become relative.[8] Since motion must be measured against some fixed reference, what is said to be moving with respect to one frame of reference can be said to be at rest from another. Second, if the world is an aggregate of colliding bodies, there can be no conception of a principle of rest, no reason for something being at rest, no sense in which something might be meant to be at rest. Even if rest were not a question of reference frame, a thing at rest would just be waiting for the next collision.

It is precisely here that Aristotle's conception of nature diverges fundamentally from a conception such as Descartes'. Returning to Aristotle's text we read: "nature is a certain source and cause of being moved and of coming to rest in that to which it belongs primarily, in virtue of itself and not incidentally" (192b21–23). We will take up this statement in four parts: that nature is a source and cause; that nature is a principle of rest as well as motion; that such rest and motion belong to a thing in a primary way; that this belonging must be understood as intrinsic to the thing.

"Nature is certain source and cause . . ." Nature is not understood here as the totality of moving things (and their laws). Rather, nature here is distinct from the things that move and rest. Nature is what is responsible for their motion and rest. A picture of colliding bodies will not help in trying to grasp Aristotle's ideas. Our oak tree and sparrow will. In Descartes' world of colliding bodies, the moving bodies themselves cause other bodies to move by impact. But it does not sound quite right to say that the moving bodies are the sources of motion since God, as it were, provided the initial push. But it might make sense to ask why acorns grow into oak trees and not sparrows. We might be on good ground asking what is responsible for the growth and development of a seed into a thing of *just this kind*.

In what way does a world of oak trees and sparrows allow for rest to have meaning where a world of colliding bodies does not? To see how, we first have to make explicit something that has been lurking in the margins. For Aristotle, motion does not mean simply (or even primarily) the displacement of a body from one place to another. Motion for Aristotle is in one sense broader than local motion, but ultimately differently focused. An earlier passage that was quoted mentioned growth, shrinkage, and alteration alongside of motion from place to place. All such changes fall under the heading of motion—*kinesis*—for Aristotle. In fact, it is often better to use "change" as the key word, rather than "motion," when thinking along with Aristotle.

But more importantly, for Aristotle change and motion do not primarily point to just any bit of flux. Rather motions must be understood as wholes. And to be understood in this way, motions must be bounded by limits. A true, whole motion must begin somewhere definite and must end somewhere definite. The motion of the oak tree begins in the acorn and ends in the oak tree. The motion of the sparrow begins in the egg and ends in the mature bird. The motions of becoming-tree and becoming-bird *come to rest* in the tree and the bird.

But don't the oak tree and sparrow continue to move? Doesn't the oak tree continue to grow and shed leaves, to increase in height and breadth, and to sway in the wind? Doesn't the sparrow eat, fly, build nests, and lay eggs? Indeed they do, and in Descartes' picture of the world all of this would be called motion. Growing, shedding, eating, and flying can all be conceived as particular instances of matter in motion. And Aristotle would not deny, for instance, that a bird in flight is a body moving from one place to another. But in Aristotle's way of seeing things, these movements are better classified as aspects of activity. An oak tree has a way of being that includes, or just is, certain modes of activity. To be a sparrow means to act— to live—in certain ways. Such activity—activity as the being of a certain (kind of) thing—must be distinguished from motion.

The acorn does not display the activity of the oak tree, nor does the sapling. But the sprouting acorn and the growing sapling are on the way toward displaying such activity. The embryo in the egg does not live the life of a mature sparrow. The hatched baby sparrow does not either. But embryo and baby bird are on the way to a particular kind of activity. *This* kind of being on the way toward something is what Aristotle means most of all by motion.

A mode of activity belongs to the acorn, even if the acorn does not yet display that activity. A way of living belongs to the baby sparrow, even though it now lives differently than it will. *Being on the way* to a certain kind of activity *comes to an end* when the thing comes to act in that way. The motions that begin in the acorn and the egg come to rest in the active lives of an oak tree and a sparrow.

NOW WE SEE why Aristotle included the phrase "that to which it belongs primarily" in the quotation above. The activity of being an oak tree is the source of motion for the acorn. We said just now that this activity belongs to the acorn. But Aristotle's phrasing suggests that we might also say that the acorn belongs to the activity of being an oak tree. There is such a way of being and to this way all acorns and oak trees belong.

Further, we can now put together the first three parts of the passage under consideration: nature as a source and cause; of motion and rest; and of belonging primarily. The constitutive activity of the life of a sparrow is itself the source and cause of the development and maturation of embryo and baby. The same activity, as the end toward which development and maturation are moving, is that in which motion thus understood comes to rest. The activities of oak trees and sparrows are different. One belongs to acorns and oak trees, the other to sparrows and their offspring.

"IN VIRTUE OF ITSELF and not incidentally." What does this qualifier add to what we have seen so far? How nature as a source and cause of motion and rest is to be understood as not incidental is clarified by Aristotle by means of an example. A doctor might cure himself and thereby be the source and cause of his own healing. But that he is, in this case, the source and cause of healing is not necessary. That is, it is only a matter of contingency that he is the doctor responsible for his healing since there are other doctors and one of them could have been responsible instead. Being the cause of one's own healing in this case is, as it were, an accident. If this is an example of an incidental source and cause, then we can get a sense of what a non-incidental one is by contrast. The non-incidental source and cause would be one where that source and cause cannot be swapped out for another.

But the example of the doctor suggests that a non-incidental cause might be found outside the thing moved and changed. If, say, there were only one doctor (and not accidentally, but by some kind of necessity), then if one were healed by a doctor it would not be incidentally so. This would turn out to be a kind of extrinsic but non-incidental source and cause.[9] Hence Aristotle's pairing of "in virtue of itself" with "not incidentally" is meant to make clear that nature as a source and cause is like the case of the doctor who heals himself inasmuch as it is the thing itself that bears the source and cause of its motion and change, while differing from the case of the doctor in not being incidental.

RECALL NOW WHY we set out to understand Aristotle's complicated statement about what nature is. The initial reason was to see in what way the distinction between natural and man-made things could be considered an obvious one. This was related to the thought that if philosophy begins from within a world—and from recognizing that one is in a world—that would mean that one begins from within a context of determinate beings.

Aristotle suggests that there is a kind of obviousness in the difference between things by nature and things by art. This obviousness is rooted in the way that the different things show themselves. The growth of an oak tree and the maturation of a sparrow just look different from the building of a bed.

Initially, we might think this difference is limited to there being a clearly-visible builder in the case of the bed, but not in the case of the tree and bird. But our combing through the four parts of Aristotle's statement about nature now suggests otherwise. Not only is there no builder visible when the acorn sprouts and grows into a tree, there is a connection between acorns and oak trees that differs from the connection between wood/nails/glue and beds. Oak trees only come from acorns. Beds can be made from materials other than wood, nails, and glue; wood, nails, and glue can be made into things other than beds.

Furthermore, what the acorn becomes is marked by a distinct mode of activity that seems uniquely intrinsic to oak trees, and only acorns can be the material beginning point for them. Even if beds possess some kind of analogous mode of activity (holding together in just the way needed to be useful as a bed), this activity seems to have an extrinsic relationship to the materials used to make a bed since the same materials can be put to other uses.

Hence we find that within the evidentness of the difference between the things by nature and things by art is the evidentness of determinate being. Natural things show themselves as *intrinsically this kind* of thing. To be oriented by means of the difference between natural and man-made things is to be oriented within a field of essentially determinate beings. Not only can we carve up the world by means of separation and collection rooted in sense experience and speech, we recognize that the natural world carves itself up by means of intrinsic, essential ways of being. Or better, a world just is a thing so carved up.

To begin philosophizing would not require one to adopt such an orientation to the world. Aristotle's view seems to be that we are all already oriented in this way. Philosophy would begin rather in recognizing that we are always already oriented in such a way. More so, philosophy would begin in being amazed in this recognition. Such recognition is not an act of opening one's eyes and mind to the world. Having our eyes open and our minds active is just our ordinary way of being in the world. Philosophy begins in catching a glimpse of ourselves having open eyes and active minds. Reflected in this glimpse of ourselves is the determinateness of the natural world.

Hence Aristotle can end his opening of Book Beta of the *Physics* with this:

> *That* nature is, it would be ridiculous to try to show, for it is clear that among the things that are, such things are many [that is, things that have intrinsic determinacy]. But to show things that are clear by means of things that are unclear is the act of one who cannot distinguish what is known through itself from what is not known through itself. (193a3–6)

■

What follows from these beginnings? What does it look like to follow upon these starting places? If these starting points are not just sites of setting out, but sources for what comes after, what do they contain that engenders what follows?

Our considerations of meaningful speech and living things both came upon the question of essential being, of something being, in some simple and ultimate way, some one thing. The principle of contradiction suggests that being must admit of determination, which was complementary to a certain way of speaking about things, namely, saying that something is *this* way and *not* that. It was left as a rather sketchy question whether some ways of being were different from others, whether some modes of determination name what a thing is simply and essentially. Our treatment of Aristotle's conception of nature suggests that there are such modes, at least for living things. Being an oak tree or a sparrow seem not to be ways of being alongside of having leaves or flying. Having leaves and flying seem to be part of what it is to be an oak tree or a sparrow.

WE WILL APPROACH the question of essential being by first taking up three other questions that spring from our starting places. These questions concern oneness, change, and incidental being. It will help to sketch briefly how these questions are already latent in what we have been through.

Both the principle of contradiction and the way living things show themselves imply oneness, though in different ways. In our treatment of the principle of contradiction, we assumed that the things said in our examples counted as real determinations: whether it is raining; whether the table is made of wood; whether Socrates is seated; whether Socrates is a human being. The principle requires that if these really are determinations of the things of which they are said, then the things cannot not be those ways. In our consideration of oneness below, we will see that certain ways of calling things one would limit what would count as real determinations. This limitation would not deny the principle of contradiction. To the extent that being is determinate, the principle holds. The question would be by what modes of determination beings actually are determined.

Each living thing shows itself strongly as one thing. This is especially true of animal organisms. How is this kind of oneness to be understood? If such oneness is genuine, what is responsible for it?

The oneness of living things highlights the second question. Living beings are not inert. Both in their proper motions toward maturity and in other ways in their life activities (for instance, an oak tree will shed its leaves in the fall), living beings stay the same while also changing. The same is true of artifacts. A knife becomes dull without being regarded as a different thing altogether. What can explain something retaining its identity while also changing?

The third question will emerge from further scrutiny of ordinary speech and will require us to ask again whether some assertions about the being of a thing differ in some essential way from others. These considerations will further develop a question we asked above: does the grammatical similarity of the sentences "Socrates is a human being" and "Socrates is seated" mask a fundamental difference?

Book Delta of Aristotle's *Metaphysics* contains a sort of philosophical lexicon. The book consists of thirty short chapters that survey the ways in which certain words are meant. Part of the approach taken in these chapters seems to be an exercise in *listening* to the variation in meaning that a word exhibits in ordinary speech. We will also see that lying beneath the surface of the way words are used is a preparation to tackle fundamental philosophical questions. The sixth chapter considers the word "one."

The second paragraph of the chapter[10] begins a discussion of the ways in which things are "called one in their own right" (1015b35). Aristotle explores three basic types of oneness—three ways of calling things one. These are oneness by continuity, oneness by a common substrate, and oneness by a common (indivisible) *logos*. The examples that follow are Aristotle's, with some attempts to amplify the points he is making as well as draw out some hidden inferences.

A BUNDLE OF STICKS is tied together. Some pieces of wood are glued together. Both of these assemblages are made up of a number of items, but nonetheless display oneness. The sticks that are tied together are one in a way that a pile of sticks is not. One measure of this, as Aristotle suggests, is that the tied bundle moves as one thing—if I try to pick up just one stick the others come with it—whereas if I grab one stick from the pile the others stay put. The same would be true of the pieces of wood glued together. As long as the glue holds, the pieces move as one. This would not be true if the same pieces were made to merely touch while resting on a table top where they might easily be knocked apart.

Aristotle points to more complex cases along these lines. Two straight lines that form an angle can be considered one. So too can a leg made up of many bones. But here Aristotle points out that we might be inclined to say that the individual lines or bones are more one than the wholes of which they are parts, because while the wholes *can* move as one thing, the parts can also move independently (while not breaking the continuity of the whole).

Let us note one feature of this kind of oneness. Reduced to its simplest notion, this way of being one has nothing to do with the kind of things that are one by continuity. Holding together—moving as one item—is the basic criterion of oneness. Indeed, if actions such as tying or gluing are the means of attaining oneness, then what is tied or glued is secondary to the strength of the bonds.

A second kind of oneness does bring in aspects of kind. One bottle contains wine, another olive oil. The wine in the first bottle is one and so is the oil in the other. The oneness here does not seem to be a matter of rigid continuity, since the fluids can be stirred around and even easily separated, say, by pouring some of the wine into a glass. However, the physical separation seems secondary to the oneness of the wine as all being the *same* wine. Indeed, one does not ask to be poured some particular bit of the wine in the bottle—any of it will do.[11] In fact, any glass of that wine will do, even if it is from a different bottle. Hence, we can see that, in a certain sense, all the wine of a particular type (say, that contained in bottles with the same label from a certain vintner from a given year) is one. (All these same things could be said of the olive oil.)

Aristotle extends this way of thinking into less ordinary considerations. What if, he asks, both wine and oil share some common underlying thing, say, water or air. If so, then, notwithstanding their sensible differences, they would possess a hidden oneness. (Before balking too quickly at this way of thinking, it might be fruitful to recall that it is also central to key areas of modern science. For instance, the groundbreaking work of James Clerk Maxwell is marked by the unification of magnetic and electric forces—which display sensible differences—as one type of thing, namely energy.) One feature of this kind of picture is that it suggests hierarchical orders of kinds, where basic underlying substrates are (somehow) differentiated into smaller subclasses. A consequence of this feature that we must keep in mind is that the greater unity would seem to be located in the more general kinds, and the greatest unity would be located in the most general kinds. On this way of looking at things then, we would be inclined to say that the oneness of things is to be found furthest from their particularity. (One example is Thales' "All is water," a pronouncement that would then claim—despite appearances—that all is one.)

ARISTOTLE INDICATES that something like this way of thinking about oneness also shows up when we classify things generically. His example is that a horse, a human being, and a dog are all called one because they are all animals. This line of thinking clearly differs from that concerning the oneness of wine in certain respects. For instance, whereas one bit of wine is as good as another, a horse and a human being are not so easily interchanged. The common feature between the two examples, however, seems to be that "animal" is one thing similarly to the wine being one thing. That is, by analogy, just as there are no criteria for distinguishing one bit of wine from another to the extent that it is the same wine, so there are no criteria for distinguishing a horse, a human and a dog to the extent that they are animals. It is in this sense that they are called one since there is no way to separate them in this respect.

We should note that this oneness of generic kinds also entails orders of hierarchy. We could also unify horse, human, and dog as mammals. Oneness of this level would exclude birds and reptiles (among other groupings). Just as when wine and oil are considered to be unified by a common underlying thing, so would mammals, birds, and reptiles be unified—made one—by means of a common genus.[12] (I do not want to pursue here further ways in which a common physical substrate might be similar to a genus. The pressing question would be whether we are to think of the genus also as a kind of underlying substrate.) Let us note also that the issue of kinds is again central. Unlike oneness by (physical) continuity, where the principle of oneness operates irrespective of kind, these other modes of oneness feature ones of a kind. In these latter modes we see that a one is not distinguished by the types of bond at work (tying, gluing, etc.), but rather in the kind of thing it itself is. Furthermore, this oneness by kind is mirrored in our speech. "Bundle" names something with a type of external binding. Wine and animal name kinds of *things*.

ARISTOTLE CONSIDERS a third kind of oneness. At first glance, this third way might appear to be only a version of oneness by genus. But Aristotle seems to set it apart, and his doing so will help us develop our main question going forward.

Aristotle says that, "all those things are called one of which the articulation [*logos*] saying what it is for them to be is indivisible into any other one revealing what the thing is" (1016a33). This is a difficult sentence, as is the passage within which it is contained. But one way of construing it—keeping with our zoological examples—is with respect to the species level as opposed to the genus level.

Looked at one way, grouping things—calling them one—as belonging to a species does not look that different from grouping them by a genus. "Those things in the field are horses" and "Those things in the field are mammals" have the same grammatical structure, and both statements gather a multitude of individuals into one group. Furthermore, horse and mammal can both be considered kinds, the only difference being the extent of the members of each class.

Yet it seems that Aristotle might consider the species and genus levels to be importantly distinct in some way. The clue is his notion of an indivisible *logos* saying what a thing is. Indivisible in what sense? In the sense that there are no differences that can be added to the *logos* that are indicative of the being of the thing.

This is certainly not true of the class of mammals. After articulating the criteria for being a mammal, further discriminations can be added that will distinguish certain mammals from others. Aristotle's frequent recourse to the two-footedness of human beings is helpful here, since that criteria makes a separation between humans and other mammals. The articulation of what-it-is-to-be-a-mammal has been divided, we might say, by inserting further criteria of differentiation.

The sentence we are considering suggests that some articulations do not admit of division in this way. Common experience might help us see what is meant. Say you see two horses in a field. They look very much alike in terms of build, but one is brown all over and the other is both brown and white. No one would dispute that the two horses are different in terms of the colors of their coats. The question would be whether this difference makes a difference in what they are.

Of course, those last three words are not adequate, because one of the horses *is* only brown and the other *is* brown and white. And further inspection would undoubtedly reveal innumerable differences between the two horses. On this way of taking the phrase "what they are" there would be no end to the divisions that could be made of articulations about what each thing is.

Hence Aristotle must mean something different when he speaks of a *logos* "revealing what the thing is." He must mean that certain differences do not count when making such an articulation, that the difference in color between our horses, for instance, should not be considered as a difference pertinent to saying what those horses are. It would suggest, then, that being-a-horse could be a way of being that is fundamental in some way. This way would not just pertain to criteria for class membership, but would be a way of being for each individual in that class. Belonging to a class and *being* that kind of thing would then be intimately tied.

■

Let us briefly probe some undercurrents of the discussions of oneness considered above, for it turns out that these ways of calling things one entail three basic ways of viewing the world. The first way of calling things one is based on things (irrespective of kind) being externally bound together. Such oneness is located primarily in physical cohesion. The second way in which things are called one is in terms of things belonging to a general kind, either in the way wine is all one kind of thing (or wine and oil together as one in being watery or airy) or in the way a horse, a human being, and a dog are all one kind of thing. This manner of oneness locates ultimate oneness at the most general or encompassing level. The third way in which things are called one is by means of names that cannot be regarded as belonging to smaller classes of things (without missing "what the thing is"). These three modes of oneness could be three basic answers to the question "Where is the fundamental unity of things in the world located?" According to the first mode, one could say that all unity in the cosmos is only a matter of external binding. That is, there would be no intrinsic unity to be found anywhere. This would be an almost-unintelligible world. Since, as we saw, such oneness is indifferent to the things bound together, an account of unity in the world of this type could only be a kind of endless description of contingent bindings of otherwise unarticulated stuff. Very little could be known about such a world and, it seems, nothing could be known about it in principle. To the second mode of oneness an intelligible order would correspond. This is especially true if we consider oneness as underwritten by means of physical substrates. In this way of considering the world, there would be as many (true) ones as there are basic kinds of substrate. Investigation of the world on this view would entail searching for and identifying these basic underlying kinds.[13] The last mode of oneness entails a view of the world in which oneness is located right at the level of discrete things. Oneness of this kind corresponds to a world constituted by things that would deserve designation as things in their own right—*independent things*.

WE HAVE AGAIN arrived at our question about essential being—the question about whether anything can be considered to be intrinsically the thing that it is right at the level of its singular, discrete being. But now our question has become couched in a more sophisticated set of considerations. Scrutiny of the different ways we call things one has resulted in basic options for how to understand the being of things. We might streamline our thinking at this point by focusing on what look like the two strongest options: a world of physical substrates and a world of independent things. The question would be: Is the world best understood as a configuration of some set of basic underlying things, or instead as the locus of discrete, namable, and independent things? Further, if it turns out that both ways of looking at the world have merit, does one ultimately take precedence over the other?

Two other questions were anticipated above: how change and identity can go together and whether all ascriptions of determination are meant in the same way. We can develop these questions quickly.

YOU BUY A new pair of boots to work in the yard. Out of the box, they are unblemished. But after a day of hard work, the leather is scratched and scuffed. No matter. Work boots serve just as well scratched and scuffed as they do when unblemished. Indeed, the boots see you through many years of yard work, until finally they can be used no more. Perhaps a hole has worn through the sole and cannot be repaired. Perhaps some stitching has finally come undone and the boots no longer protect your feet. Nevertheless, in the years between, as the boots gradually wear out, you regard them as the same boots. You might say to your spouse when lacing them up one morning, "These are the same boots I've been wearing for years." Your spouse might respond, "I remember when they were brand new. They don't look the same to me."

Both of you seem to be saying something true. In one sense the boots are the same, or more precisely, we might say they are the "same ones." No one has snuck into your closet and switched your boots for another pair. There is *something* that remains the same about the boots you put on year after year. But in another sense your spouse is right— the boots are not the same. They have changed.

Aristotle traces this kind of scenario in the first book of the *Physics*. He calls our attention to two ways of looking at change. On the one hand, change must be located in a relationship between contraries, or between presence and absence. When the boots come out of the box they are *uns*-cuffed. After a day's work, they are scuffed. Aristotle would say, "The scuffed *comes from* the unscuffed." Only where there is a lack of scuffing can scuffs come into being.

But to say that where there was a lack of scuffing there now is scuffing, there needs to be more than the unscuffed. There must be something that is at first unscuffed and then scuffed. Indeed, when you take the boots from the box, you wouldn't regard them simply as unscuffedness. Rather—if it even crossed your mind!—you might think, knowing what will happen after a day's work, "There are no scuffs yet on these boots." They are *things* that are unscuffed. Hence Aristotle also says that change requires an underlying thing, a bearer of the change. Perhaps you have a friend who says when you show him how scuffed your boots have gotten after a day's work, "Well, it's not the *boots* that are scuffed. It's the leather." Your friend wouldn't be wrong, even if you are (rightly) not inclined to give up the claim that it is in fact the boots that are scuffed.

There seem then to be two ways to regard the persisting thing that is the locus of change. On the one hand, there are the boots. The boots remain the same boots despite getting scuffed. On the other hand, there is what the boots are made from—leather, rubber, thread, and glue. The leather gets scuffed, but is not obliterated. The rubber wears down, but not all at once. The boots remain because the materials underlying them persist.

OUR EVERYDAY LIVES are saturated by interactions with discrete things. But not only do we identify discrete items as a matter of practicality—"Can you pick up a gallon of milk on your way home?"—our ways of speaking privilege such items. "That horse is white," is something we would say. "That white is a horse," we would not. "That white thing is a horse," we also might say, but not, "That horse thing is white." Aristotle would have us pay attention to the fact that we have such restrictions on meaningful speech.

Aristotle would also have us acknowledge that these restrictions on our ways of speaking carry a certain understanding of different modes of being. How so? Here we can return to the first paragraph of Aristotle's discussion of what is meant by "one," which we skipped over earlier. That discussion begins, "One is meant in one sense of what is so incidentally, in another sense of what is so in its own right" (1015b16). We traced above the range of ways that one is meant "in its own right." What does Aristotle mean when he says we call something one incidentally? His example: Corsicus and educated are one. In recognizing that Corsicus is an educated man, we recognize a kind of unity. This is captured when saying, "Corsicus *is* educated." But we also recognize that the unity here is not "in its own right." Why? Either because we recognize in general that not all human beings are educated, only some are; or because we remember a time when Corsicus was not educated. That he is now and that he and his education are one in some way cannot mask the accidental character of this oneness.

Putting these two things together, we start to get a picture of different modes of being—a picture implicit in our ways of speaking and in our attitudes about items in the world. The picture that emerges is one in which certain words pick out things about which things are said— "That *horse* is white"—while other words name things said of something else—"That horse is *white*." In many cases, we recognize that what is said of something is not said of necessity. A brown horse standing next to the white one shows us that white need not be said of horses. Horse and white going together in this horse is incidental.

But also, Aristotle will insist, being white, for instance, is nevertheless a way of being. There is *being* in the being-white of the horse. Indeed, there are many such modes of being: size, location in place or time, relation to something else, undergoing something. He also insists, however, that such modes of being are always referred to or depend on some primary thing. The *table* is five feet long. The *bird* is in the tree. *John* is taller than his brother. The *water* is being heated.

■

We find ourselves with a puzzle. There appear to be two prime candidates for the very being of things. On the one hand, things seem best understood in terms of their material. Such materials can be considered either in the way leather underlies boots or in the way water, as a possible elementary material, might underlie wine and oil. This understanding of being is able to grasp all perceptible things in a comprehensive way. On the other hand, things seem to be what they are not in terms of the material underlying them, but rather in terms of an indivisible *logos* saying what they are. Being a boot seems to be more than being made of leather, rubber, and glue. It seems to be even more than leather, rubber, and glue put together in a certain way. That is, the being of a boot *as* a boot seems not to be rooted primarily in the arrangement of the materials, since this arrangement itself seems subordinate to and guided by the purpose the boot is meant to serve. Hence, in a way, the being of a boot is not a material thing at all. Needless to say, what is true of a boot seems even more true of living things, where the underlying materials are not simply arranged in accord with some use or plan or design, but seem to merge fully with the active being of the living thing.

When material is understood as true being, all material things seem to have an equal share of being. But when being is understood in terms of an indivisible *logos*, materials that are not arranged in some definite way seem to fall outside of true being. (For instance—to borrow one of Aristotle's examples—a misshapen lump of bronze would seem to be less of a being than the same lump after being given a spherical shape.) Hence the puzzle. Since both ways of understanding being seem to have merit, settling definitively on either of them would close off a path that seems to provide insight into being. But simply stopping at this point and saying both are true would seem to leave us without an adequate understanding of being since the two are not fully compatible. We will search for a more adequate understanding of being in the opening chapters of Book Zeta of Aristotle's *Metaphysics*.

WHEN ARISTOTLE speaks about things like tables, birds, and human beings and wants to indicate their priority and independence, he uses the word "*ousia*." In common usage in Attic Greek, this word is used to refer to one's property in the wide sense of wealth or estate. It indicates in a broad way "that which is one's own."[14] "*Ousia*" is also a form of the verb "to be." These remarks help explain why Aristotle uses "*ousia*" to refer to nameable, independent things. On the one hand, as we have seen, there are reasons to think that being-a-horse is more the horse's "own" than being-white, or being-six-feet-tall, or being-in-the-field. On the other hand, this "ownness" is not really a matter of possession. That is, it does not seem that there is something existing independently that possesses horse-being alongside whiteness, being six-feet tall, and standing in a field. Rather, horse-being seems to *be* the ground of the thing's independent being.

This helps us understand why Aristotle says at the end of the first chapter of Book Zeta that "the thing that has been sought both anciently and now, and always, and is always a source of impasses, 'what is being?,' is just this: what is *ousia*?" (1028b5). On the one hand, being seems to be said most forcefully by *ousia* words. On the other hand, other ways of saying being are either referred to or seen as dependent upon the things named with *ousia* words. The point is not that all ways of being are reducible to *ousiai*, but that understanding *ousiai* will be the key to unlocking the question of being. This is indicated earlier in the chapter when Aristotle says that just as we understand something best when we understand what it is in this strong sense (i.e., as a horse, rather than as white), so we will understand best what, say, white is when we understand *its* whatness, that is, the whatness of color. These questions, however, pertain to questions about how a science of being is possible and how that science must be pursued. Our goal here is more modest. Our question will not be how understanding *ousia* can ground a science of being, but how there can be *ousiai* in the more primary sense at all. That is, if indeed it is right to think that tables, birds, and human beings have genuine independence, what explains this independence? Our investigation of Aristotle's thought will culminate with a sketch of his opening moves in pursuing this question.

THE MAIN OUTLINES of this pursuit should now be evident to us. Consider that in the examples of *ousiai* above I left out one type of thing that we have been dealing with, things like water. When we say "The water is being heated" we say something very similar to "The horse is white." Both water and horse serve as the primary referents with respect to being-heated or being-white. Without the water and the horse, it seems, there would not *be* being-heated or being-white. But we have also seen that water and horses differ in one crucial way: all water is one thing in a way that all horses are not. This difference comes out again in our ordinary ways of speaking. While we would say "There are many horses in the field," we would not say "There are many waters in the glass."[15] Hence we have returned again to our questions about oneness. We will want to ask first whether the kind of oneness displayed by horses really exists, or instead only the kind of oneness seen in water. Two questions follow—questions that can be asked independently of each other: If the oneness of discrete beings is genuine, does this mode of oneness take priority over the oneness of material substrates? If the oneness of discrete beings is genuine, what is responsible for that oneness?

WE WILL DO WELL to look directly at the first two sentences of the second chapter of Book Zeta. The first reads:

> Now being-independent seems to belong most evidently to bodies (and therefore we say that animals and plants and their parts are *ousiai*, as well as natural bodies such as fire and water and earth and each thing of that kind, and as many things as are either parts of these or made out of them, out of either some or all of them, such as the cosmos and the parts of it, the stars and the moon and the sun). (1028b9–14)

Aristotle begins with what seems most evident. The evidentness of independent being attributed to bodies mentioned here seems to point back to the first mode of oneness we considered earlier. Independence is displayed by bodily things inasmuch as they cohere and move as one thing. The mark of independence here is the physical coherence and continuity of the bodily thing. This is why both wholes and their parts can be said to be independent things. Both the whole and its parts cohere and move as one thing in certain respects. The "we say" in the quotation seems to indicate that this is a common way of (implicitly) understanding being. It is common, I think, for good reason. Many bodily things do display this kind of coherence. The material world does not show itself to us as being radically in flux. Instead we see very many things holding themselves together just fine. It is not in the spirit of Aristotle's thinking to simply undercut or doubt the way that the material world presents itself.

However, the next sentence is:

> But whether these alone are independent things or
> there are also others, or just some of these are, or some
> in addition to some other things, or none of these but
> something different, must be examined. (1028b14–16)

While the philosopher must be attentive to and show a certain deference to what is commonly evident, he must also be prepared to set aside that evidentness in light of further inquiry. This attitude is not one of skepticism and doubt, but rather a stance of rigorous openness. The rigor shows up in the completeness of the options run through in Aristotle's sentence. It could turn out that all, some, or none of what at first seem to be independent things really are. The openness is indicated by declaring the necessity to look into which it turns out to be.

Aristotle tells us about other kinds of things one might encounter in carrying out such an inquiry. He mentions that some think the limits of bodies, namely, surfaces, lines, and points, are more independent than the bodies themselves. Others, such as Plato and Speusippus, claim that there are independent things entirely apart from bodies (for instance, forms and mathematical things) and that these may have a higher degree of being than perceptible things. Aristotle concludes this preamble to the investigation proper by saying,

> Now about these things, what is said well and what not, and what *ousiai* are, and whether there are any apart from the perceptible things or not, and in what way these are, and whether there is any separate independent thing, and why and in what way, or none at all apart from perceptible things, must be examined by those beginning to sketch out what *ousia* is. (1028b28–33)

THE THIRD CHAPTER of Book Zeta initiates the comprehensive and fine-grained study of the question "What is *ousia*?" One can begin to get a sense of the demands of reading Aristotle's text at this point, for Aristotle sets out four ways in which *ousia* is meant "most of all." These are as underlying thing, as genus, as universal, and as the nearly-untranslatable *to ti en einai*, which in this passage Sachs renders as "what [a thing] keeps on being in order to be at all." A couple of things are worth noting. First, it must be recognized that Aristotle is not simply thinking things through in his text, from the things most evident to more remote conclusions. There is such a movement in the text, but it is combined with a prior gathering of various lines of thought and a sifting of them in order to offer an organized presentation (even if this organization is sometimes difficult to discern). So one way of seeing the task of reading this text is to endeavor to catch up with where Aristotle already is. Second, this requires wrestling with Aristotle's vocabulary. I have thus far tried to locate Aristotle's thinking in ordinary lines of thought and will continue to do so in what follows. But philosophical writing often requires untypical uses of language, and comprehending the need for and meaning of such uses is a constant requirement of philosophical reading. Hence, third, the remainder of this chapter, while following along with parts of Aristotle's text, is not meant as a commentary on the text as such. Partly this means that we will not pursue any discussion of three of the four ways in which *ousia* is meant. We will only consider the one that has emerged already for us, *ousia* as underlying thing.

To repeat, we have encountered two ways in which material can be understood as that which underlies a thing: in the way that leather underlies a boot and in the way that water might underlie wine and oil. In Book Zeta, Aristotle considers yet another way to think about material as an underlying thing. We can take up Aristotle's new line of thought as a kind of thought experiment. In the two ways of considering material that we have already seen, there is a common feature. When leather is made into boots, there are aspects of determination that are added to the leather that make the material boot-like and not just "raw" material. By analogy, we might think that water as underlying material is further determined in some way to become either wine or oil. The thought experiment would go like this: What if we proceed in the reverse direction and remove (in thought) the determinations that are added to the material? Considering the boots, for instance, we could ignore the boot-like aspects and train our minds just on the leather. Likewise, we could think about the common wateriness of wine and oil. But what if we continued this way of thinking, for raw leather is not completely undetermined stuff? Leather has certain sensible qualities that make it different from rubber, for instance. But might there be a common underlying material for leather and rubber—a material to which determinations are added to become leather and rubber? Here our two ways of thinking about material converge, for perhaps this removal of determinations will always lead us back to some set of elemental materials, each with certain determinate features, but no longer removable.

Aristotle suggests, however, that the momentum of our thought experiment must take us further. A multitude of diverse elemental materials with different determinations cannot withstand the dissolving power of our thinking. For even if this diversity is in some factual way irreducible, our *thoughts* can go further; the logic of the thought experiment has not reached its conclusion. Indeed, the line of thought that leads from leather, rubber, wine, and oil to elemental materials can continue. If elemental earth and water differ by means of sensible determinations, we can ask what underlies *those* determinations. Our thinking has been premised on the notion that something capable of receiving determination underlies determinate things. If we remain true to our premises, we must see that the terminus of our line of thought is an underlying thing *lacking all determination*. This is where such thinking ends up.

Let us take note of some strange features of the termination of our thought experiment. We have arrived at a seemingly contradictory entity. On the one hand, this ultimate underlying material is meant to be tangible stuff. We can start with leather as the being of a boot, for instance, since the tangible character of the leather seems to be what allows the boot to be an independent thing. But, on the other hand, we end up with something that is not tangible at all, that is, something that can only be thought. We can have no tangible experience of something that lacks all determination, but we can think about a kind of ultimate substrate that would be the thing able to receive determination. So, we might want to ask whether this thought is a coherent one. What does it mean to think a total lack of determination? Haven't we seen indications above that thinking and determinateness go together? Don't thinking and meaningful speech require that things are, and are said to be, this way and not that? Rather than this substrate-lacking-all-determination being the ultimate substrate, might not our line of thought suggest it is nothing? Isn't it only nothing that lacks all determination?

ARISTOTLE DOES NOT linger over these questions and immediately indicates the insufficiency of thinking about being as underlying thing in terms of ultimate material. He says that it is "impossible" that *ousia* is material "for also to be separate and a *this* seem to belong to an *ousia* most of all" (1029a28–29). We have tried above to capture what Aristotle says here by talking about discrete, nameable things. Indeed, we have seen from a number of angles that we not only think about things in terms of common underlying materials, but also—and often more primarily—in terms of discreteness and particularity. Three ways seem most evident: in our everyday dealings with useful artifacts; in the individuation displayed by living things; and in the way we single out such things as grammatical subjects in speech. An investigation of being that did not take up these matters would be a poor one indeed.

The sentence quoted above continues: "on account of which the form [*eidos*] and what is made out of both [i.e., form and material] would seem to be *ousia* more than would the material [alone]." Here, for the first time, Socrates' word has entered our discussion of Aristotle. We have, then, one final task: to understand why *eidos*-talk must come into our investigation. Understanding this need will then allow us one final insight: that philosophy must have a second beginning.

■

The detailed investigation into form begins with Chapter 7 of Book Zeta. The chapter opens with a summary of some of what we learned about Aristotle's understanding of nature and living things above. In particular, Aristotle emphasizes here that natural beings come into being out of and toward some nature. As we saw, oak trees and sparrows each come out of and move toward some nature. Only oak trees generate acorns, and only acorns become oak trees. Only sparrows generate sparrow eggs, and only sparrow eggs become sparrows. But we now see more clearly that living things must be referred to some material. Acorn and egg are only potentially oak tree and sparrow. Such potency, we have come to see, is just the fundamental feature of material taken generally. The qualification to be made here is that particular materials are not unlimited in their potency. Just as not every type of material can be used to make a shoe, so not every material has the potency to be an oak tree or a sparrow. As we have noted frequently above, the way in which the material sources of living things differs from the materials of artifacts is that the material sources of living things seem tied exclusively to one kind of being, whereas the materials used for artifacts can be used to make different kinds of things.

We will return to consider living things one final time, but only after a detour of great consequence. We have seen that the coming into being of living things seems to unfold from within the things themselves. A contrast was noted in this regard with man-made things, where a maker must work on materials to bring the artifact into being. Aristotle thinks we can learn something about *ousia* by looking more closely at the making of artifacts.

WHAT IS INVOLVED when someone with house-building skills builds a house?[16] Aristotle suggests that our answer to this must be in line with this general statement: "So of the process of coming-into-being [of artifacts], one part should be called thinking [*noesis*] and the other making [*poiesis*], the thinking starting from the source [*arche*] and from the form [*eidos*], and the making starting from the completion of the thinking" (1032b15–16). Let us try to understand two aspects of this statement: that making something (like a house) requires thinking; and that the thinking must be completed (in some way) before the making can begin.

Aristotle's argument for why making requires thinking seems, on the one hand, to be implicit in what he says about how such thinking unfolds, and, on the other hand, to be a matter of introspection—to the extent that we all experience this unfolding when *we* make things. Aristotle says that things are made according to a form, pattern, or knowledge "in the soul," and that "by form [he means] what it is for them to be." For instance, the house builder is able to build a house because he has the form of a house in his soul. We might say, he knows what a house is. But as we saw above, what something like a house is can be considered in two rather different ways. On the one hand, it can be thought of as a certain arrangement of materials. On the other hand, and more primarily it seems, a house can be understood in terms of its use.[17] These two ways of understanding what a house is can nevertheless be brought together. Why is the house built on a solid foundation; why are rigid and durable materials used to make walls and roof; why are the rooms sized this way and laid out that way? The answers to all of these kinds of questions can be referred to the primary understanding of the house as a form of shelter and place for living. *Only if* the house is made from materials with certain properties, secured and arranged in certain ways, can they serve as—*be*—a house. I think Aristotle expects us to assent to two things here. First, he seems to expect that we are familiar with what is outlined above. We have all endeavored at some point to put materials together to make something, and it is unavoidable that such an endeavor has the two aspects highlighted: that there is a primary goal (for example, some object of utility) at which we are aiming; and that we have to consider which materials and which means of arranging those materials will conform with that goal. Second, he seems to expect our assent that the thing at which we are aiming is a form, something knowable, and that we possess this form within ourselves. Furthermore, he seems to expect assent to the claim that in actually trying to make the thing aimed at we must think through the considerations about materials and their arrangement. If Aristotle is right to expect assent to all of this, we can conclude that form and thinking go together and that whatever else form might be it is a thinkable thing.

We can also readily see in what way thinking must be completed before making can begin. Why does the house builder, for instance, begin building by digging a trench? To lay the foundation. But why is *that* the first thing to be done? Because the house will rest on it—it must be in place before the walls can be erected. The house builder must think from the last thing to be achieved—the fully-formed house—to the first thing to be undertaken—securing the foundation. Making, Aristotle means to stress, must be seen as the thoughtful arrangement of materials.

But since thinking about materials and their arrangement is subordinated to the form as the primary what-it-is of a thing, all making finds its ultimate source in the form itself. The skillful maker carries out what is already contained in the form.

IF ARISTOTLE IS RIGHT that the guiding source for making something is a form residing in the soul, what kind of thing is this form? Aristotle proceeds by showing us one thing that it is not: something made. What does he mean by this?

In the opening sentences of Chapter 8, Aristotle recapitulates that when something comes into being it does so "by the action of something" (*the house builder when he is building*), "out of something" (*the bricks and wood*), and "becomes something" (*a house*). In the continuation of the sentence, Aristotle shifts to the example of fashioning a bronze sphere: "just as one does not make the underlying thing, the bronze, so too one does not make the sphere, except in the incidental sense that the bronze sphere is a sphere, and one makes that" (1033a28–30).

With this assertion the world begins to look strange. We set out above to find the being of things. By taking seriously the integrity of discrete, nameable things, we were not content to comprehend being in terms of material alone. Looked at another way, we were compelled to seek an explanation of how discrete, nameable items can each be one. *But the oneness of such things has now become two.* From the ordinary view, a bronze sphere, a house, and a shoe are each one thing. Our inquiry, however, has refracted such ones into two aspects, a material aspect and a formal aspect. I use the word aspect here in order to indicate that whatever this kind of twoness is, it cannot be the kind of twoness displayed by two bronze spheres, two neighboring houses, or a pair of shoes. Why is this? Two points from our inquiry show us why. First, we have seen that an account of the being of things in terms of underlying materials cannot fully account for the oneness of discrete, nameable things. (Shoes cut from the same piece of leather can be called one in a way that undercuts their separateness.) Second, one meaning of being an independent thing (an *ousia*) is to be a member of a class or kind. There seems to be a close connection between oneness and nameability. The analysis of making suggests a way of understanding this connection. Forming materials makes them something in this stronger sense. Providing form—where form means what something is—seems to confer oneness on the thing. That the pieces of leather that make up this shoe and that shoe came from the same larger piece is somehow left behind and made less important once two discrete shoes come into being. We might see this by noting that we have not simply moved from a one (larger piece of leather) to a two (the shoes); we have moved from having nothing discrete and nameable (the leather is not so much a this as material for being made into something) to having discrete, nameable things (the shoes). Hence the real wonder here is not that one piece of leather can be cut in two, but that *where there was not something (or scarcely anything), something came into being.* And it did so according to a form. In some way, it seems that the form/material twoness of a formed thing *is* its oneness.

The argument for why a form cannot be something made is of a familiar type to readers of Aristotle. The point is essentially this: if making requires material and form—

if making requires in every case the *out-of-which* and the *something*—and if a form were made, it too would have to be made out of something and according to some form. If a form could be made, it would have to be made from material and form. Two kinds of problems arise. On the one hand, it is not clear what the material of a form could be. On the other hand, there would be no end to such makings, and therefore no principles of making. Material and form were appealed to as what allow for something to come into being, as what explains what making is. So if form is also something made (and the same argument would apply to material) then the possibility of explaining making in terms of form and material falls apart. As Aristotle would say, an explanation must come to a stop somewhere.

That bronze can be made into a sphere is well within ordinary experience. But is sphereness an object of experience in the way that bronze spheres are? Isn't being-a-sphere a different kind of being than bronze? And isn't being-a-sphere something, ultimately, that we grasp only with the mind? If being-a-sphere means being-equidistant-from-a-center (in three dimensions), isn't that manner of being said irrespective of the material? I can see and touch a bronze sphere, but can't I only think its sphereness? Furthermore, is the sphereness of the bronze sphere different from the sphereness of a marble one? Don't we say that the bronze and marble spheres have the same form? Isn't it the case that *there is* a form that all spheres possess?

If we answer these questions affirmatively, what follows? First, we will have affirmed that there is a manner of being that is immaterial and intelligible. Being intelligible will have been affirmed as a kind of being. Second, what is intelligible will have been affirmed as the being of discrete, nameable things more so than the material. We will have approached this thought: To be is to be intelligible.

IN THE FIRST CHAPTER, we said that the search for forms was both a grounding and a provocation. The same is true here. Arriving at the thought that being is grounded in the intelligible is not the end of thinking. It is instead a new beginning and a provocation to further thinking. We will do well to sketch out some of the questions provoked by this new beginning. Our questions will lead back from the example of the bronze sphere, past the example of house building, to our thoughts about oak trees and sparrows.

WHAT IF IT turns out that bronze spheres are a bad example for thinking about form as the being of things, or that we were misled in some way? Some of the force of the remarks above springs from the uniquely intelligible character of mathematical things. It seems that we are able to grasp fully the whatness of mathematical objects through their definitions. There is an intelligible transparency to mathematical thinking that gives it its character. It seems, as well, that this transparency might allow us to separate cleanly (in our thinking) the formal aspect of a bronze sphere from its material aspect, since the formal aspect can itself be treated as a kind of object.

Are we able to do the same thing when thinking about, say, houses? Does house have the same kind of intelligible character as sphere? Some of the difficulty in answering these questions comes, perhaps, from ambiguities about how to grasp properly a form with the mind. We noted above that, with respect to things like houses, the physical configuration of the materials, while in some sense the form of a thing, should probably not be construed as the ultimate form. The ultimate form would be something captured not by apprehending a shape, but by articulating something in speech. So maybe the difference in intelligibility of house and sphere is not one of kind, but one of degree. Perhaps we can grasp the form of a sphere within the shape more readily because its articulation in speech is simpler than that of a house.

I raise these questions not to try to settle them, but to indicate how the investigation must shift once it moves into questions about intelligibility. The questions shift from questions about things to questions about what is knowable in things. Or, perhaps more simply, the questions shift to what is knowable as such.

We said above, *there is* a form of a sphere. But what does this mean? How are we to understand the "there is" in this assertion? Is sphereness some kind of entity apart from bronze or marble spheres? Again, the study of spheres in geometry might suggest that in doing geometry we get our hands on the forms of geometric objects themselves. But do we? What would have to be asked in order to answer that question?

The question is perhaps even more pressing with respect to houses. Does it even make sense to posit houseness as a form apart from particular, material houses? Doesn't the very notion of a house, in a way, refer to a material thing? If being a house is at bottom being a place for the sheltering and cultivation of human living, must not a house be a material thing? If so, what does it mean to say we grasp the form of a house as what is intelligible in houses if there is no such thing as a house apart from particular houses?

Perhaps our reliance on the making and being of artifacts is responsible for these thorny questions. Perhaps this was the wrong path to pursue in taking up the question about the being of discrete, nameable things. After all, the independence of artifacts is questionable on a number of fronts. First, the formation of raw materials into proper artifacts comes from the outside. The forms of artifacts are not intrinsic to the materials, as we have noted often above. Second, the forms of artifacts are always referred to human needs and desires in some way. As things that are useful for or desirable to us, they do not exist on their own, as it were, but depend on our needs and desires to give sense to what they are. And, third, artifacts cannot take care of themselves. They wear out, fall apart, and otherwise degrade with time and use. Just as they require an outside maker, so do artifacts require something outside themselves for their maintenance. These considerations suggest that artifacts might be poor candidates for *ousiai* after all.

It appears again, then, that living things should be commanding our attention, for unlike artifacts, living things do display independence in these ways: they are self-generating; what they are is not subordinated to use or desire; and they maintain themselves. It seems as if the investigation of *ousia* should have been focused on living things all along. Among perceptible things, these seem to be the truly independent beings.

Before jettisoning our work too quickly, however, we would have to ask whether Aristotle is correct that all coming into being has the same requirements. Our focus above was on human making as the model of coming into being. In that model, the agent that sets the material in motion— forms the material—is outside the material. Furthermore, the form is located in the soul of the maker. But Aristotle says that the same things are required for the coming into being of natural things as well: agent, material, and form. The difference would only be in whether these things are intrinsic or extrinsic. Our question, then, would be whether the extrinsically related elements of human making can provide insight into the coming into being of living things. In particular, we would want to know whether the introspective evidence of forms in the soul can be carried over by analogy to living things. Put bluntly: Do living things possess intelligible forms? Is there something at work in the acorn/oak tree and egg/sparrow that is of the same sort as the sphere or house in the soul of the craftsman?

■

The turn to form is a second beginning for the philosopher. Determinateness can no longer be taken either as a built-in requirement of ordinary speech or as simply manifest in the way the world shows itself. The source and ground of determinateness has now itself become the question.

In a way, however, this second beginning is a reprise of the first. The move toward investigating determinateness in terms of intelligible forms is but a recasting of the inherent intelligibility of ordinary speech. And the inclination to hold out living things as the beings that most fully exhibit independence is a recapitulation of emphasizing the obvious difference between living and man-made things.

This second beginning is the first beginning played in a different key. This repeating of the first beginning in the second will only bother us if we think that philosophy is meant to get beyond beginning. What if philosophy is only meant to comprehend the meaning of how it has already been able to begin?

SUM

To create concepts.

I take the first number 7, and, as I take the fingers of my hand as an intuition for assistance with the concept of 5, to that image of mine I now add the units that I have previously taken together in order to constitute the number 5 one after another to the number 7, and see the number 12 arise. (*Critique of Pure Reason*, B15–16)

WHAT COULD BE more common than adding numbers like 7 and 5? Maybe you are having a dinner party and are expecting seven guests. Then another friend calls to say she and her family can make it after all. That will mean five more. Almost automatically you do the sum in your head: there will now be 12 guests. You *know* that 7 and 5 make 12.

Knowing here means something like "memorized that $12 = 7 + 5$." But what is the basis for regarding what is memorized as correct in the first place? Or, how could you confirm that 12 is indeed the sum of 7 and 5? The quotation above gives one description of what lies behind the memorized answer: counting up from 7 to 12 using your fingers!

Perhaps your young daughter asks how many people will be coming to the party and you use the moment to practice some addition with her. You say, "Well, there were seven people coming, but now five more will be. Let's see how many that is." You have her hold out seven fingers and show her five of yours by opening your hand. Then you close your hand and start opening it again, one finger at a time, counting, "Eight, nine, ten . . ." With the fifth finger you reach 12 and you both agree—there will be 12 guests.

The goal of this chapter will be to contemplate—following the account offered by Immanuel Kant in his *Critique of Pure Reason*—how this all-too-familiar procedure is possible. Some of what we will encounter is already announced in the quotation above: why counting relies on *intuitions* and *concepts* and why adding is a form of counting. Some is implicit in the quotation, most especially the expectation that we can recognize objects as separate things, as *ones* (e.g., fingers). And especially, we will want to ask how both you and your daughter can agree that 7 and 5 *must* make 12, that the sum is arrived at by necessity—for the experience of adding numbers is nothing without this element of necessity.

■

You and a friend are building a large table together in your woodshop. The tabletop has been assembled and needs to be set aside so that you can begin work on the base. You need help moving the tabletop and say, "Can you help me move this? It is too heavy for me to lift alone." You know this because you just tried. If asked why it is too heavy for you to move, you might answer in various ways: you are not strong enough; it is too large; it is made from very dense wood. Such answers are all based on the relation between how strong you are and how much the tabletop weighs—if you were stronger, if the top were smaller, or if it were made from wood that was less dense, you might have been able to handle it alone.

What if instead of being asked why the tabletop is too heavy for you to move alone, you were asked—perhaps by a child—why the tabletop is heavy at all. You might begin to answer by saying, "All bodies are heavy." In answering this way, Kant will say that you have made a judgment, and in making a judgment that you have thought something through concepts, here the concepts of body and heaviness. Note one feature of this judgment: its origin is in experience. The concept of a body itself—we are following Kant here—does not include the idea of weight or heaviness. That is, we will not arrive at the idea of heaviness by inspecting what is meant by "body." It is by lifting things that we come to know that bodies have weight. Hence the assertion that "All bodies are heavy" is one that attaches something found in experience to the concept of a body.

To make the base for the table, a length of wood needs to be cut to six feet. Now imagine you are asked why it is possible to make a cut in the wood. Again, certain kinds of answers could be given that relate the qualities of the wood to the tools in the shop. The wood is softer than the blade on your saw. The blade is sharp. The motion of the saw blade against the wood separates the wood from itself. But if the child asks how it is possible at all that the wood can be cut, you might answer, "All bodies are divisible." The conversation might get a little tricky at this point. How do you know that all bodies can be divided? Is your answer based on your experience cutting things? Is there perhaps some body that is so hard it cannot be cut? And what do you mean by divisible anyway? Does divisible mean "able to be cut"? Maybe with some reflection you come to see that what you really meant by "All bodies are divisible" is that they all have parts. And not parts in the sense that they are all assembled out of parts, but that they can be described in terms of parts: right and left parts; a top and a bottom; an inside and an outside. If this is what divisibility is, then ascribing divisibility to bodies does not rely on experience. How so? Because the very notion of a body includes occupying a space and thus being extended. Extension and divisibility are "characteristic marks" of bodies and hence are included already in the concept itself.

WHAT, THEN, is a concept? Let's try to untangle the sentence below:

> All judgments are [. . .] functions of unity among our representations, since instead of an immediate representation a higher one, which comprehends this and other representations under itself, is used for the cognition of the object [. . .]. (A69/B94)

"Representation" is here a primitive term. We can take it to mean anything that is present to the mind. What is Kant's sentence saying about what we are doing when we proclaim (i.e., assert in the form of a judgment) "All bodies are divisible"? We can begin by saying what we are not doing. We are not attending immediately—simply, directly—to something in the mind. For instance, we are not merely bringing the notion of a body, or even all bodies, to mind. (Not only are we not doing this in forming the judgment, I think we will come to see that in Kant's view, we cannot *ever* simply entertain concepts individually and immediately.) Rather, the judgment, somehow, unifies things in the mind. The somehow is by "comprehending this and other representations under itself." How does this apply to "All bodies are divisible"? Here "all bodies" is comprehended under "divisible." According to Kant's claim we need to note two aspects of this comprehension. First, "divisible" stands higher than "body." "Higher" here indicates that one concept is wider in scope than what is comprehended under it. We think about bodies by means of a representation that can comprehend "all bodies" and "other representations under itself." For instance, a stretch of time is not a body, but it is divisible.[1] Second, by comprehending all bodies under a higher representation, I unify the implicit multitude contained in the phrase "all bodies" by passing over to "divisible." I think something about *all* bodies at once in asserting them to be divisible.

We are now in a position to say more precisely what a concept is. The perhaps surprising key to understanding what a concept is for Kant is that concepts find their proper role as the predicates of judgments, not as their subjects. Typically we talk about having a concept of this or that, as if it were a singular thing possessed by the mind. Take the concept of a body. What does it mean to say that I understand something by possessing this concept? And what do I possess in possessing this concept? Is it a word? Do I understand something by saying "body" to myself? What if I picture a body in my mind? Do I understand something by such picturing? In contrast to the sense that concepts have significance in their mere possession, Kant asserts that concepts have significance only in their *use*. And this use, as we saw above, is the comprehension of other representations under them. I can comprehend something about bodies by deploying the concept of divisibility. "Divisible" is a concept only inasmuch as it can comprehend under itself other representations. We think through concepts, by passing from the object of thought to a higher representation.

"Body" is also a concept. That it is can be affirmed by showing it to be a possible predicate in judgments. Kant writes,

> The concept of body thus signifies something, e.g., metal, which can be cognized through that concept. It is therefore a concept only because other representations are contained under it by means of which it can be related to objects. It is therefore the predicate for a possible judgment, e.g., "Every metal is a body." (A69/B94)

IT IS ONE THING to assert "Every piece of metal is a body"; it is another to say "*This* thing in front of me is a piece of metal." In the first assertion, my thinking does not relate immediately to any particular object. The phrase "every piece of metal" already sets my thinking at a distance from particular pieces of metal. "Every piece of metal is a body" passes through two concepts. Not only does it think pieces of metal through the concept of body, it thinks any piece of metal I might really encounter through the thought "every piece of metal."

When I declare the thing in front of me to be a piece of metal, this is also thought through a concept. I think something about the thing in front of me by passing over to a concept that "comprehends this and other representations under itself." The thing becomes more than a bare *this* by passing over to "metal." But in doing so, I recognize—indeed, rely on the fact—that this is not the only piece of metal in the world. It is by "falling under" the heading "metal" that the thing gains in determinacy.

But in this case, unlike the first, there is an element of immediacy. "This thing in front of me" is not a concept. I cannot employ "this thing in front of me" as a predicate in a judgment. Nothing falls under "this thing in front of me" in the way that "this thing in front of me" can fall under "metal" or in the way that "metal" can fall under "body." What then is named by "this thing in front of me"? Kant says it names something *given* to me, something that I *receive*. But what is it that is given and received? Notice that the question is not precise enough. What if one said, "The *piece of metal* is given and received"? I might respond (with my newly acquired Kantian vocabulary!), "No. Seeing the thing as metal was mediated by a concept. I want to know what I received directly, without the passage through a concept." Is there an answer to this question? Won't all answers be expressed in the form of a judgment, that is, a sentence of the form "The thing received directly is X"? Won't the X be some concept under which the thing would fall, and hence the thing would be grasped mediately, not immediately? That something is received immediately seems necessary to assert. What that something is seems, in principle, beyond articulation.

WE HAVE a small puzzle here that we won't be able to solve just now, but should be noted. The thrust of the reasoning above has been that concepts have their proper role in the work they do as predicates. This work has a double aspect. We have been emphasizing the way that what is named as the subject in a judgment is brought under a concept wider in scope, and in doing so the subject is determined—and hence thought—in some way. We should recall in addition that in bringing the subject under a concept, Kant claims that we bring unity to our representations. For instance, "all bodies" and "every piece of metal" name multitudes, but these multitudes are gathered into one thought when something is predicated of them. The multitudes are thought as one.

But our discussion has shown that concepts are also used in the subject position of judgments to name the object to be determined and thought by means of the judgment. How can we use concepts as subjects if their proper role is as predicates? We might be able to make sense of this if we can show that the way concepts operate in the subject position of judgments is at bottom the same as the way they operate as predicates, that is, by gathering a multitude under them and bringing unity to that multitude. This will indeed turn out to be the case, although it will take some time to see how and why. It is already evident, as noted above, that in forming a thought such as "every piece of metal" I reach out in thought to an indefinite multitude of objects that are gathered together by means of the concept of metal.

WE HAVE ARRIVED by means of our inquiry about concepts at one of Kant's fundamental teachings—that our minds possess two basic capacities, one of receptivity and another of spontaneity. Through intuition we receive objects; by the active employment of concepts we comprehend objects. Kant is quite clear, however, that it is only the coordination of these powers that produces cognition.

> Neither of these properties is to be preferred to the other. Without sensibility no object would be given to us, and without understanding none would be thought. Thoughts without content are empty, intuitions without concepts are blind. (A51/B75)

THERE IS NOTHING more ordinary than picking out nameable items in the course of a typical day. While building the table with your friend, you need to drive some dowels into holes that have been drilled in the base, and you ask your friend to fetch a mallet. Your friend returns with a rubber mallet and you say, "Sorry. I meant the wooden one." How can you identify both tools as mallets? How can you distinguish the rubber mallet from the wooden one? Kant would say, by means of concepts. Why? Why can't we just say that, for instance, mallets *look* different from other tools and rubber looks different from wood? The catch in the question is that it is already asked in terms of concepts. Mallets are recognized as mallets by means of certain characteristic marks. Hence it is not to deny that mallets indeed do look different from other tools; the point is that in happening upon *this* tool and recognizing it as a mallet one recognizes it as containing, we might say, mallet-marks. I can't identify a thing as a mallet without having already understood that if something is to be a mallet it must have those marks.[2] When scrutinizing the thing in front of me I do not simply await the thing to declare its identity. I do something. I hold it up to a standard. I ask myself under what overarching concept the thing falls. I come to things in the world already armed with concepts. I do not apprehend mallets immediately *as* mallets. To apprehend the thing in front of me as a mallet is always to pass over from its characteristic marks to the concept. I perceive the mallet as a mallet through thinking about it.

And so it would be also in distinguishing the rubber from the wooden mallet. These materials would have their own characteristic marks, marks that would allow a standard of judgment to be applied. Despite rubber and wood being kinds of materials, our experience of them—the experience of discernment—happens through concepts. And we can even allow some looseness in this scenario. Usually it might be enough to distinguish the rubber from the wooden mallet by means of color. But maybe the head of the wooden mallet has been painted and is now black like the rubber one. A squeeze will reveal a difference. But again, for this difference to count as a criterion for distinguishing between rubber and wood, you must already have included those marks as elements of a conceptual standard.[3]

It will take rather more digging into Kant's text to see why he thinks our experience must, as it were, include concepts all the way down.

■

Kant says that number, as a "concept of the understanding," is "a representation that summarizes the successive addition of one (homogeneous) unit to another" (A142/ B182). Let's approach this definition with an example. Say you have gone apple picking. After picking apples for a while, your basket has gotten rather heavy. You wonder how many apples you have picked so far. How do you figure this out? You count them, of course! Perhaps you do this by first dumping the apples on the ground and placing them back in the basket one by one. As you place them, you say to yourself, "One, two, three . . ." At some point, all of the apples are back in the basket and you have reached some definite number, say, 23. Kant's suggestion seems to be that the number 23 is constituted by your counting of the apples, hence the word "summarizes." We might think that the number 23 exists in itself and is reached in your counting of the apples. Kant, rather, is saying that 23 is a summary—a summing up—of a process. The process is addition itself, the addition of units one after another.

Let us note that this way of understanding numbers might seem deeply strange if we look closer. If Kant is really saying the numbers themselves are summaries of a process that unfolds successively, then this means that numbers are dependent on time. It takes time to add things up one after another, and if the number itself is a summation of this adding up, then number has a temporal aspect. We will return to this below.

What is meant by "homogeneous units"? In our example it was the apples. But it could have been any number of things: trees in the orchard, rows of trees in the orchard, miles driven to the orchard, minutes spent picking apples, and so on. In each case we would have in view, on the one hand, things we regard as each being one—apples, trees, rows, miles, or minutes; on the other hand, we would take in a multitude of such things. Oneness and multitude go together here. If the ones do not show themselves as each one—if, say, they start to bleed into one another—then there can be no multitude. But, Kant's suggestion seems to be that multitude is not yet number. I see that there are many apples in the basket, but this is not yet for me the apprehension of a definite number of apples.

This way of putting it might make us doubt Kant's understanding of number, for now we might say, "Even if *I* have to count them in order to know how many apples are in the basket, *there is* some definite number of apples there before I count them." It is just this seemingly reasonable declaration that Kant is questioning. Kant questions that there is a number of apples before they are counted up and summarized. Taking him at his word, Kant seems to be saying that the apples cannot accomplish this summarizing, but we can.

You count the apples in the basket; there are 23. You count the rows of trees in the orchard; there are also 23!

You say, "There are the *same number* of apples in my basket as there are rows of trees in the orchard." What can be meant by same number here? Would Kant agree with the statement? I think he would. His agreement is already indicated by his calling a number a concept.

We saw above that a concept was able to be used as a predicate in a sentence, and that in occupying the place of the predicate it had wider scope than the subject (it was a "higher" concept). For instance, "divisible" is wider in scope than "body," hence "All bodies are divisible," but not "All divisible things are bodies." We can see that the same holds for numbers. "There are 23 apples in the basket." "There are 23 rows of trees in the orchard."[4] The number 23 is wider in scope than apples or rows of trees. The number 23 can comprehend these "and other representations under itself." But this should be no surprise since Kant said that as a concept a number relies on "homogeneous units." This is an entirely general notion. While it is indeed true that "23" *summarizes the successive addition* of the apples, it not *as apples* that they are successively added, but as homogeneous units. The number 23 can apply to apples and rows of trees equally because, strictly speaking, the number is always a number of units and not things.

Unity is conferred on each apple or row by means of a concept. It is as if, in perceiving each item, we silently uttered "This is an apple, and this is an apple, and this is an apple . . ." The concept of an apple is put to use in these judgments by making it possible to pick out discrete items. Pick out from what? Some reflection would suggest—if we limit ourselves to vision—that sensibility is presented with nothing more than a field of colors. In one sense, when I open my eyes, I see only this field—a mere spread of sensible stuff. I don't see things. And yet it also seems true to say that our experience of perception is the perception of discrete things and not just a spread of colors. The apple on the ground *stands out* as something separate from the ground, and discrete unto itself. Kant contends that this standing out is not something passively received by me. Rather— somehow—I must actively draw the outline of the apple in order for it to stand out. This outlining is the work of concepts. Hence, having units available for counting, and thus number, too, depend on concepts.

With this we are ready to plunge into the depths of Kant's understanding of the mind and its relation to the world. The transition will be aided by noting how this new question—the question of how perception includes concepts—follows upon the discussion of concepts above. Our examples of judgments included "Every piece of metal is a body," and we noted how this judgment brought unity to the multitude of pieces of metal by bringing them under a concept.[5] In judgments like "This thing in front of me is metal" we noted that what is given indeterminately is determined by means of the judgment, by bringing the given under a concept. But we did not cast this determining in terms of unity, although we did note that if a concept shows up as the subject of a judgment there should be a hidden act of unification in that concept. We now have a candidate for what is unified in such judgments: whatever it is that is given in sensation. Color is one kind of thing given in sensation. What is not given is the boundary between the apple and the ground. Only a field of color is given in sensation. As a field, it is color all the way across.[6] In drawing the outline of the apple, however, I set apart a portion of what is given. The next step is the crucial one, for while the outline, as it were, has put a boundary around part of the field, there is still multiplicity within the boundary. In order for what is contained in the boundary to count as one thing, that multiplicity too must be gathered up. This gathering up is also not given. We must do it ourselves.

■

We do not count concepts. We count items that are apprehended as units by means of concepts. Counting units is somehow an interplay of sensible and intellective powers. The following—somewhat monstrous—passage gives a compact statement of what these powers are and what is required of them in order to make counting possible. *It turns out that what makes counting possible is the foundation for what makes ordinary experience itself possible.*

> All appearances contain, as regards their form, an intuition in space and time, which grounds all of them *a priori*. They cannot be apprehended, therefore, i.e., taken up into empirical consciousness, except through the synthesis of the manifold through which the representations of a determinate space or time are generated, i.e., through the composition of that which is homogeneous and the consciousness of the synthetic unity of this manifold (of the homogeneous). Now the consciousness of the homogeneous manifold in intuition in general, insofar as through it the representation of an object first becomes possible, is the concept of a magnitude (*Quanti*). Thus even the perception of an object, as appearance, is possible only through the same synthetic unity of the manifold of given sensible intuition through which the unity of the composition of the homogeneous manifold is thought in the concept of a **magnitude**, i.e., the appearances are all mag-

nitudes, and indeed **extensive magnitudes**, since as intuitions in space or time they must be represented through the same synthesis as that through which space and time in general are determined. (B202–3)

Tackling this passage will require us to explore three fundamental aspects of Kant's understanding of human cognition: our possession of pure forms of intuition; the fundamentally synthetic nature of consciousness; and the role of pure concepts in conscious experience.

IMAGINE YOU have been given a set of data—for instance, monthly rainfall amounts in your town for the last year— and are asked to provide a graph. Two facets of this scenario will require our attention. First, without actual data, you cannot produce the graph. Without measurements, a graph of monthly rainfall amounts is a mere idea. Second, there is a choice of *form* for producing the graph. Monthly data could be represented in either a line graph or a bar graph, for instance. Hence, on the one hand, the form in which the data is presented is not given with the data itself; and on the other hand, you must have the forms of such graphing schemes already at hand if you are to order the data according to some such scheme. Line graph and bar graph are forms of ordering data. While there cannot be an actual graph without real data, the data remains graphically formless without some formal scheme.

Kant argues that the intuitive[7] aspect of experience is analogous to the scenario above; not only must something be given to the mind, we must possess a form by which what is given can be ordered.

The effect of an object on the capacity for representation, insofar as we are affected by it, is **sensation**.

That intuition which is related to the object through sensation is called **empirical**. The undetermined object of an empirical intuition is called **appearance**.

I call that in appearance which corresponds to sensation its **matter**, but that which allows the manifold of appearances to be ordered in certain relations I call the **form** of appearances. Since that within which the sensations can alone be ordered and placed in a certain form cannot itself be in turn sensation, the matter of all appearances is only given to us *a posteriori*, but its form must all lie ready for it in the mind *a priori*, and therefore be considered separate from all sensation. (A20/B34)

The crucial phrase for us is "allows the manifold of appearances to be ordered in certain relations." Kant does not provide a robust argument for why there must be a form by which and into which sensations are received and ordered. The reasoning seems to be along the lines of our analogy to data and forms of graphing. Just as I must know what a bar graph is before I can order my data within that form, so "the receptivity of the subject to be affected by objects necessarily precedes all intuitions of these objects" (A26/B42) and such receptivity must be a form of ordering. Kant says we have two such forms of receptivity, space and time. Space is the form of "outer sense" and time is the form of "inner sense." Unlike rainfall data, which we can order by means of different formal schemes, we cannot manipulate the "matter" of our sensations independently of the forms by which we receive them (for example, we cannot experience color that is not spread across an extended space). But we might be able to get some access to the bare form of order hiding underneath.

Now IMAGINE a space filled with objects. Remove all sense qualities from the objects (for instance, light and color, hardness and weight). Try to think of all the bodies in the room only as things that occupy a space. Finally, remove the objects altogether. Does anything remain? If so, is it removable, too?

Kant has four things to say about this thought experiment: that we cannot imagine that there is no space; that our sense of space does not come from experience; that space is not a concept; and that space is encountered as a given magnitude. We will try to draw these four things out of the thought experiment.

We can say the words "There is no space," but when Kant says, "One can never represent that there is no space" (A24/B38), I take him to mean that it is impossible for us to *picture* the annihilation of space. Perhaps this seems circular, but I think the circularity would be part of Kant's point. Picturing things is necessarily spatial. We have a sense of what it means for things to be spatial. This sense differs from the purely logical use of the understanding: anything that is represented conceptually can be logically annihilated by attaching "not" to it.

If Kant is right about this, it dovetails with his second assertion: our sense of space cannot be learned from encountering things in space. In his short exposition of this point, Kant says that things being "outside and next to one another" cannot be equated with being "different." Mere difference is a conceptual distinction and can apply to non-sensible things. For instance, necessity is different from contingency, but neither can occupy a position in space. Hence difference alone cannot be the ground of knowing what "in different places" means. Kant suggests that the space that one cannot annihilate in the imagination is the ground for any representation of things that are outside and next to each other, that is, in different places. He writes, "this outer experience [of objects in space] is itself first possible only through this representation [of space itself]" (A23/B38).

And this representation cannot be the representation of a concept. As the predicate of a judgment, a concept represents a characteristic mark of a possible or given object. In the latter case, the given object is judged as one instance of an indefinite multitude of objects that can display that mark. For instance, "This body in front of me is divisible" thinks the singular thing by means of the mark of divisibility, a mark that other bodies can display. "All bodies are divisible" thinks about no particular body, but the judgment does imply a multitude of discrete items, all of which would contain a common mark. To anticipate the contrast Kant wants to draw with space, we can note that it does not sound right to say that each body is a *part* of divisibility. Divisibility is not divided up through being predicable of each and every body. That is, there may be many things that are divisible, but these many things share a common mark and are not parts of a whole.

Spatiality, however, is not a characteristic mark of spaces. Spaces *are* parts of space. Kant writes,

> [O]ne can only represent a single space, and if one speaks of many spaces, one understands by that only parts of one and the same unique space. And these parts cannot as it were precede the single all-encompassing space as its components (from which its composition would be possible), but rather are only thought **in it**. It is essentially single. (A25/B39)

Finally, since space differs from concepts in this way, we see that it is encountered (in us) as a "given magnitude."[8] Spaces do not fall under the whole of space as bodies fall under divisibility as a characteristic mark. Spaces are "within" space itself. I think our sense of "within" here is of a piece with the considerations above. Being able to grasp the difference between something that can only contain its members within and as parts of itself, and something that can be a characteristic mark of a multitude, *just is* an indication that our intuition of space is different from our use of concepts.

What is given—for instance, color—is given in intuition. Colors are not given independently from a form of ordering. On the one hand, colors are given always as spread out, as patches of color. On the other hand, different colors are given as next to each other. Being spread out and next to one another is a condition of outer sense. Even though we cannot imagine a color without its spatial form, Kant contends that we can still come to see that a form of ordering must reside in us as a ground for receiving the "matter" of color itself. This is what Kant means when he says that space is an *a priori* intuition.

These reflections also help us understand what Kant means by appearances. Consider again the analogy to graphing data. While it is certainly possible for us to gather the data without graphing it (in a list or spreadsheet, for instance), imagine for some reason that we could only ever encounter the data already graphed. In that case, our rainfall data would "appear" to us by means of some form. The graphically presented data would have a double aspect inasmuch as we could distinguish its "matter" (data) from its "form" (graphing scheme), but only the two together yield something that appears. Under this fictional scenario, the raw data would be inaccessible to us (we could not know what the data is "in itself"); and the graphing scheme is only a form of ordering. Hence, Kant's position is that all empirical experience of things in the world is of appearances in this sense: *something* is given to us, but since it is received by means of a form of ordering, we do not have experience of the something in itself.

THE CONTENTION that space is not a feature of things as they are in themselves, but a subjective form for ordering appearances is challenging. (I have not asked you simply to accept this; I mean only to indicate the outlines of Kant's position.) But Kant will also try to convince us that "time is nothing other than the form [. . .] of the intuition of our self" (A33/B49). How can time be a form for ordering appearances if it is the form for intuiting oneself? What does intuiting oneself even mean?

YOU AND A FRIEND are having coffee at a café. The two of you are sitting together at a table. This is a description in terms of time. You order drinks and then the waiter brings them. This, too, is a description in terms of time. Objects must exist and events must happen either simultaneously (*at the same time*) or in succession (*at different times*).

IMAGINE AGAIN a space filled with objects. The image turns out not only to be something spatial, but something temporal as well. One cannot help but regard the objects as occupying the space at the same time. Any changes imagined in or between these objects must be ordered in terms of before and after. Hence time is a necessary condition for ordering objects and events in relation to one another. Even the intuition of space itself, regarded as a given magnitude that contains all of its parts within itself, is conditioned by time. The parts of space must be grasped as being simultaneously within the whole of space. For these reasons Kant says that "[t]ime is a necessary representation that grounds *all* intuitions" (A30/B46) [my emphasis]. Space is not time; but neither space nor things in space can be intuited without time.

But how do we get from time as a form of ordering objects and events to time as the form of *inner sense*? Why inner? The answer is already contained in the preceding paragraphs, but requires us to pry apart the spatial and temporal aspects of ordinary experience. (The word "aspect" once again is meant to indicate that space and time are somehow really distinct in experience, but also that experience is a cohesive whole—it is not made up of spatial elements and temporal elements.) Kant writes, "[t]ime cannot be a determination of outer appearances; it belongs neither to a shape or a position, etc." (A33/B49–50). When you and your friend are seated together at the café, the togetherness can be construed either spatially or temporally, indeed must be construed both ways to capture the usual sense of the word. If you sat at one table and your friend sat at a different one across the room, we might say that you were in the café together, but not that you were seated together. "Seated together" has a spatial meaning, something like "at the perimeter of the same table." But "together" must also mean "at the same time." If you sat at a certain table in the café yesterday and your friend sits there today, we could say that you both sat in the same space, but not that you were seated together. Hence your togetherness has a temporal aspect that cannot be gleaned from any description of spatial position.

Since spatial descriptors cannot capture the "at the same time" feature of togetherness, simultaneity cannot be a feature of "outer sense," that is, it is not a form of ordering objects that are outside of me inasmuch as they are outside of me. Rather, "before," "at the same time," and "after" refer to the ordering of representations in me. Put simply, my thoughts come one after the other. Whether things are regarded as simultaneous or successive must begin from[9] the fact that my thoughts come to me in a certain form of ordering. Analogously to our apprehension of objects in space, Kant insists that this form of ordering must reside in us as a condition for thinking at all, for having thoughts. I do not gain a sense of time from my thoughts coming one after another; coming-one-after-another is a form of ordering in which I receive my thoughts.

Hence, our thoughts themselves must be understood as a kind of *appearance*. We might be tempted to think that this is the case because, for instance, we cannot think without engaging in something like silent, but internally audible, speech. Even if this is the case, Kant's claim is more austere: it is from the character of their form of ordering itself that our thoughts are appearances. Time is not an act of spontaneity; it is a form of receptivity.

WE NOW HAVE some grasp of what is meant by the first sentence of the monstrous passage we started with: "All appearances contain, as regards their form, an intuition in space and time, which grounds all of them *a priori*."

■

When counting apples, you get distracted and forget which number you have reached. So you dump the apples out again and start over. Why? Why does forgetting require that the counting start back from the beginning? This question places before us an issue we have been avoiding until now: Kant's claim that a number is a "representation that summarizes" successive addition. This claim, at least in terms of our experience of counting, seems entirely reasonable.

> If, in counting, I forget that the units that now hover before my senses were successively added to each other by me, then I would not cognize the generation of the multitude through this successive addition of one to the other, and consequently I would not cognize the number. (A103)

But what is true of counting must be true of conscious experience in general:

> Without consciousness that that which we think is the very same as what we thought a moment before, all reproduction in the series of representations would be in vain. For it would be a new representation in our current state, which would not belong at all to the act through which it had been gradually generated, and its manifold would never constitute a whole, since it would lack the unity that only consciousness can obtain for it. (A103)

There are two issues here, one of which is rather straightforward; the other is harder to grasp. To grasp the more straightforward issue, consider what must be happening in your mind when watching a sporting event, say, a soccer match. The match is tied 1-1 and is in the final minutes. You are apprehensive because your team must win in order to advance in the tournament. Suddenly your team scores a goal and takes the lead. You jump from your seat in excitement and celebration! What makes watching the match an occasion first of apprehension and then of celebration? Memory makes this possible by giving what is happening in the moment context, and this context is rooted in time. We can see this at a number of temporal scales. With a score of 1-1, the final minutes take on urgency within the context of what has occurred earlier in the match. You have seen both teams play well. Remembering this keeps the outcome especially unclear. Perhaps a star player from your team has just been ejected from the game. Remembering this makes the remaining minutes of the match more tense. But there is a larger temporal context within the tournament as a whole. The need for your team to win in order to advance must also be remembered if it is to contribute to your apprehension. An even larger temporal context would give the match other levels of significance. Perhaps your team was eliminated in previous years at this stage of the tournament. You badly want them to advance further this year! Perhaps there is a longstanding rivalry between the two teams in the match. The point is clear: without holding these various contexts in the mind they cannot bear on the present moment. And all present moments must be regarded in relation to some context to have meaning and significance.

This is what Kant means by "reproduction in the series of representations." The mind must continually exercise a power that reproduces things that have been present to the mind in order to make experience possible. I think we can see now that this must be the case even in ordinary perception. For instance, in watching the soccer match, you watch as one player passes the ball to another. In order to perceive this as a passing of the ball you must regard the event as a whole, as beginning with the kicking of the ball by one player and ending with its reception by the other player. And the movement of the ball—occupying different places on the field in different moments—connects the beginning and end as a continuous and cohesive event. The moments of the pass must be recalled continuously and gathered together in order for you to perceive the pass as an event.

KANT REFERS to the exercise of this power as the "reproductive synthesis of the imagination." He means by this nothing more than what we sketched above: the mind's need and ability to recall and make a whole out of things which have already passed through the mind. But Kant also names the exercise of this power as one of the "transcendental actions of the mind." Why transcendental?

As our remarks above suggest, ordinary conscious experience would be impossible without the context provided by "reproductive synthesis." At issue is not how this synthesis is possible in terms of, say, how the brain works (although this could be investigated). Neither is it a question of whether we experience our minds being active in this way. Kant is not asking us to seek confirmation of such synthesis by means of attentive introspection. Rather, Kant is making this kind of claim: *without* reproductive synthesis, ordinary conscious experience would be impossible.

This is what Kant means by "transcendental": anything which must be in place in order for experience to be possible. On this basis, we can begin to understand why Kant characterizes his project in the opening sections of the *Critique of Pure Reason* as an attempt to establish the "conditions of the possibility of experience."

We can also see in retrospect that space and time as forms of sensible receptivity are also transcendental features of the mind (not transcendental actions, but rather transcendental conditions for receiving the matter of sensations). In emphasizing above that space and time are necessary because some form of ordering is necessary for receptivity, we were already engaged in transcendental philosophy.

Should we have wondered earlier why space and time seem self-evidently to be wholes—one space, one time? Kant thinks this needs explaining, and that it too will be explained by means of the imagination. In this case, however, it is as *productive* that the imagination is at work.

Consider again the suggestion that space and time are given magnitudes. In our discussion above, the givenness of space and time was approached largely through attending to our own imaginations and by considering how space and time differ from concepts. Thinking about space, for instance, seems to lead us to a picture of an unbounded space that contains any limited spaces we might imagine. We do not apply space to objects by means of judgments; rather we find that objects are ordered in one (seemingly given) space.

But we have not laid emphasis on the wholeness of space and time. Strictly speaking, space is the form of ordering appearances as outside of one another and time is the form of ordering appearances as simultaneous or successive. Is it necessary that there be one space within which outer appearances are arranged? Is it necessary that appearances are ordered within one time? The transcendental answer is yes. Without space and time being unique wholes experience would not be possible. For what if space and time were not unique wholes? What then? A mundane example might suffice. You are at home and need to get to the store. How do you know that in moving from your living room to the garage, into your car, and then out of your neighborhood and across town to the store, you can get there? Is it something you learn from experience, that your house, neighborhood and town are all part of one space? The point might be even clearer with time. In terms of one's own experience, things must have happened in the past, be happening now, or be yet to happen. Furthermore, there must be continuity between things past, present and future. One way to construe the possibility of multiple times would be to imagine them as running on parallel tracks. But such an image suggests that if someone were somehow to jump from one track to another, there would be not only a break in the continuity of time, but a kind of fracturing of experience. If events from the first track of time could not be carried over to second, could the "someone" even be one consciousness?

However, even if the need for wholeness is granted, why is an act of synthesis required? Why aren't space and time just, as it were, automatically wholes? I think the reason is that for both space and time their essential feature is that their parts are *outside of* one another. They are what allow appearances to have relations of here-and-there and before-and-after. Even as forms for the subjective ordering of appearance, we might say that it is not in the nature of space and time to hold together. Something else is required to hold space and time together. This something else is the productive work of the imagination. Prior to any ordinary experience, the mind must have always already gathered up space and time into wholes.[10]

UNITY CANNOT come to experience passively; unity is always an achievement, a gathering up and holding together.

We can now understand most of the second sentence of our monstrous passage: "[Appearances] cannot be apprehended [. . .] i.e., taken up into empirical consciousness, except through the synthesis of the manifold through which the representations of a determinate space or time are generated, i.e., through the composition of that which is homogeneous."

■

But that sentence continues ". . . and the *consciousness* of the synthetic unity of this manifold" [my emphasis]. In the two passages quoted in the previous section Kant says similar things. He says not only that I must remember that I have been counting, but I must remember that the counting has been done *by me*. This follows from the general claim that we must be *conscious* of the fact that what is reproduced by the imagination has been reproduced. This emphasis on consciousness takes us to the deepest point of Kant's reflections on the conditions of the possibility of experience.

Consider how a television screen works. Unlike a celluloid film projector, which provides the illusion of moving images through a series of still photographs (each frame stopped momentarily as it moves through the projector), the "frames" of a television image are built up continuously by changing the colors of pixels one at a time, starting at the top left of the screen and moving across each row of pixels and then progressively down the screen. The whole screen is refreshed (usually) 60 times each second. So, when the refreshing of the pixels reaches the last one at the bottom right of the screen, for a moment a complete "still" image is on the screen. In the next moment, though, the refreshing begins again at the top left. While this is happening, the pixels further along hold their colors until it is their turn to be refreshed. Hence, we have here a process where every pixel "remembers" its color for 1/60 of a second and each pixel's 1/60 is staggered in an ordered sequence with all the others. One sixtieth of a second is a very short stretch of time, but it is nevertheless not a mere instant—it has some duration. This is enough to use it as an analogy for the reproductive imagination: each pixel "reproduces" its color for 1/60 of a second before being refreshed.

In a single pixel, then, we have an analogue of the reproductive imagination: each pixel must retain its color for some duration to provide context for the pixels that are changing their colors before and after. But of course these discrete pixels are not scattered about willy-nilly. They are gathered together in a certain form prior to being lit up. This would be the analogue of the productive imagination: a gathering together of a "pure manifold" into a whole that makes possible the presentation of sensible material. (Notice that the "productive" ordering of the pixels is in place even before the television is turned on. There is a *unified* "form of ordering" prior to there being sensible "matter" [i.e., lit pixels].)

It is precisely here, however, that the analogy will simultaneously break down and highlight Kant's next assertion. The screen functions and is pre-arranged in such a way as to present coherent images. But these images are nothing *for it*. A television doesn't *watch* television. If the television screen were to provide an adequate analogy to consciousness, it would have to be able, as it were, to look at itself and regard the images constituted by the pixels as its own.

Here, however, we reach one of the hardest thoughts Kant requires of us. What would "own" mean in the sentence above? We might say, "It would mean that the television was conscious." But that is what we want to understand, what consciousness is. It seems that in some way having a sense of what it would mean for representations to be "one's own" just is what consciousness is.

If being conscious ourselves is in some way the touchstone for understanding what consciousness is, it is not sufficient for understanding what the principles of consciousness are. For that, transcendental reflection is required. (That is, again, reflection on the necessary conditions for experience.) Thus far we have come to see that both pure forms of intuition and reproductive and productive imagination are required to make sense of ordinary experience (which is conscious experience). The last requirement for making sense of conscious experience is that not only must the presentation of a unified manifold be able to be regarded by me *as* mine,[11] *I* must be unified. *I* must have always already gathered myself up as one consciousness.

There is something bizarre in this formulation. If there is an I that gathers up the self, then *that* I would be the ultimate unity that grounds consciousness. Such an I, it seems, would not be something gathered, but a power of gathering. Empirical consciousness would be a manifold gathered by such an I, but this I seems as if it could be a simple "ungathered" power. The problem is that this power, too, must be mine. It is not enough that there be a power of gathering, that power must be held by me. But then what looked as if it could be simple appears once again as multiform. *Consciousness, however, requires unity.* How can we get out of this loop? Kant thinks the only way to explain the possibility of consciousness is to posit an *original synthetic unity* as the ultimate principle of consciousness. This is a truly weird idea, but one Kant thinks we cannot do without: a gathered-gathering that is pure, that (somehow) precedes[12] all other gathering (this would include both the *a priori* gathering of productive imagination and the empirical gathering of sensations into conscious perception). *Of* this ultimate gathered-gathering there can be no consciousness—it makes consciousness possible. But transcendental reflection allows us to recognize its necessity: without original synthesis I cannot be a conscious being. Kant's transcendental argument for original synthesis is a form of self-knowledge.

■

Philosophical thinking requires us, in the end, to kick away the support provided by examples, images, and analogies. This is not to say that we become untethered from what is immediate and ordinary. In our present investigation, both ordinary experience of objects and events and our ability to add numbers remain the ground and touchstone for our thinking. But as we have seen, our thinking has issued in notions that are far from ordinary.

We have encountered now two *pure* principles of human cognition: pure intuition and pure original synthesis. Neither is simply available to us for inspection. Both are approached only through the movement of thought itself.

Once productive synthesis of imagination and pure synthesis are introduced, it is clear that we have no way to experience pure intuition. We saw above that as forms of receptivity, space and time cannot achieve their own unity; a principle of unity is posited in productive imagination. But now we see further that any introspective exploration of spatial representations must ultimately be grounded in pure synthesis, since such introspection is *conscious* introspection. The challenge that Kant presents to us is to see if we can come, nevertheless, to regard pure intuition as more than a mere whim of philosophical fancy, or, worse, an empty bit of verbiage. While certainly no ordinary thing, we are asked to see pure intuition as something real. If we are to do so, it can only be through taking up the whole sweep of Kant's thinking.

This requires, however, seeing pure forms of intuition in a double way, as simultaneously real and ideal. Transcendental philosophy produces a kind of unavoidable parallax. Seeing space and time as real conditions of experience requires also seeing them as ideal, where ideal means they are "nothing as soon as we leave aside the condition of the possibility of all experience, and take [them as things] that ground the things in themselves" (A28/B44). Negotiating this parallax is a uniquely philosophical challenge.

The purity of original synthesis is even harder to grasp than that of space and time. It is worth stressing that despite the talk of "I" and "me" at the end of the last section, transcendental synthesis has nothing to do with personality, with me as different from you. The original synthesis that grounds consciousness must be seen as the principle of *consciousness as such* and not as a kind of central kernel that makes someone a unique being. Uniqueness of personality falls entirely within the realm of appearances. Personality is one of the things that is *for* consciousness, not its basis. As with pure intuition, the movement of Kant's thinking asks us to find in original synthesis something really there, but not in the manner of a mere thing.

And so it is with all philosophical thought that reaches out toward principles. Principles so conceived are not "abstract." If there are ultimate principles that ground and explain ordinary experience, the principles must be real. To say that they can only be encountered in thought does nothing to diminish their reality.[13]

■

We should gather up once more what we have encountered in the previous sections. Read again the beginning of the passage we are attempting to comprehend:

All appearances contain, as regards their form, an intuition in space and time, which grounds all of them *a
priori*. They cannot be apprehended, therefore, i.e.,
taken up into empirical consciousness, except through
the synthesis of the manifold through which the representations of a determinate space or time are generated,
i.e., through the composition of that which is homogeneous and the consciousness of the synthetic unity of
this manifold [. . .].

It should be clear now that these sentences relate to the
three principal powers of our cognition: space and time as
pure forms of intuition; the unity of the intuitive manifold
through productive imagination; and consciousness as ultimate unity through original transcendental synthesis. In
principle, then, consciousness is the (implicit) consciousness of the unity of all of these transcendental elements.

WHAT HAPPENED, though, to that other way of express-
ing the unity of cognition, namely, that it was a unity of
intuitions and concepts? Indeed, the first considerations
of this chapter led to the suggestion that ordinary experience—which we can now understand as a complex unity
of consciousness—is *wholly dependent on concepts*. Ordinary
awareness, it seems, "picks out" objects through concepts.
And, it was said that concepts make thinking possible by
unifying a multitude under characteristic marks. This was
fairly clear in judgments like "All bodies are divisible,"
where the multitude was the collection of all bodies. It was
less clear in judgments like "This is an apple." Indeed, it
was in order to understand how the concept "apple" works
in such a judgment that we took up the passage we are still
untangling.

We do not yet have an answer, but we have what could be an answer if one thing falls into place. The preceding sections have shown how consciousness must be understood as a unity of the manifold of intuition. This manifold is not an empirical manifold, that is, it does not contain the "matter" of sensations. It is only a unity of the form of ordering what is given in empirical intuition. Our investigation will coalesce if it turns out that even this unity of pure intuition is dependent on concepts. And so it is. The original synthetic unity of intuition in consciousness accomplishes this unity by means of pure concepts. Our ability to pick out objects such as apples within the manifold of empirically given intuition is grounded in the concept of a magnitude.[14]

APPLES LYING on the ground are just instances of any kind of discrete object encountered in the sensible manifold. Like any visible object, each apple takes up space. Or, we might say, each visible thing occupies some part of the extended manifold of outer intuition. It would seem at this point in our investigation that *it just needs to be so*. Since space is the form of ordering in which perceptible objects must be given, and since something more than the form must be given (e.g., color), objects must be given as extended. We left off earlier, however, with the thought that objects are not simply given. Instead, it seemed that we had to draw a boundary around them by means of a concept. But this boundary-drawing presumes already a unity of the manifold in consciousness. Hence we are led back to where we were with the analogy of the television screen: it is not enough to have pixels that can be lit up; they must be unified into one manifold, and that unity must be a conscious unity. Consciousness is thinking through concepts, so somehow the conscious unity of space must be a unity through concepts.

The clue is once again contained in what has come before. We have said a number of times that space and time are given as magnitudes. We saw above that the unity of these magnitudes was not a feature that accrued to them simply as forms of ordering intuitions. Rather, that unity had to be conferred upon them in one sense by productive imagination. But while we see and imagine all space as one space, what does it mean to *understand* that space is a magnitude? What does thinking have to do with our sense of space as a single given magnitude? Kant will say that thinking and understanding are involved because our sense of space in consciousness is mediated by the concepts of unity, plurality, and totality.

These three concepts are the ones that fall under the heading of quantity (which in this context can be considered as synonymous with magnitude) in the table of categories. All three are required to think about any continuous or discrete magnitude. How so? In our ordinary conception of number, the three concepts are clearly at work. In the number 7, we find: unity in the ones (units) that are collected; plurality in there being more than one unit; and totality in taking the plurality all together. The number 7 as a quantity requires reference to all three concepts. It is a little trickier to see that something like this must also be the case in regarding, say, a plane figure as a magnitude. It might seem that being a magnitude is simply immediately evident in a spatial figure since it covers some extent of space. I think we can see that this is wrong by filtering this hunch through the concepts we are considering.

If being a magnitude were something immediately given, it seems it would have to be thought (brought to consciousness) under the concept of unity—only a unit can be given all at once. But magnitude and quantity answer the questions "How much?" and "How many?" This means that to apprehend a plane figure as a magnitude is to (at least implicitly) regard it as containing a plurality, as measurable by means of some unit. (Unlike with discrete numbers, this unit would be arbitrary. Furthermore, any arbitrarily designated unit for measuring extended magnitudes must itself be regarded as a magnitude. This is one way of regarding the continuity and infinite divisibility of geometric figures.) And the boundedness of the figure means that this plurality is taken as a totality. A whole movement of thought, it seems, is hidden behind the seeming immediacy of seeing spatial figures as magnitudes.

These considerations suggest that the consciousness of items in intuition as magnitudes resides in thinking about what is given in intuition by means of certain concepts. Again, though, we have a case where the given cannot be separated *in consciousness* from what is thinkable in it. Part of our challenge and part of Kant's point is that what is given in intuition must be given as magnitude. This is why concepts such as unity, plurality, and totality are said to be pure concepts: they are not derived from experience; they make experience possible. These concepts are the initial basis for consciousness of what is given in intuition.[15]

Finally, we should note once more that this pure relation between intuitions and concepts is a transcendental achievement: it precedes in principle all empirical application of concepts to intuitions (e.g., comparing colors in my visual field to the marks contained in the concept of an apple.) The remainder of our passage will now be clearer:

Now the consciousness of the homogeneous manifold in intuition in general, insofar as through it the representation of an object first becomes possible, is the concept of a magnitude (*Quanti*). Thus even the perception of an object, as appearance, is possible only through the same synthetic unity of the manifold of given sensible intuition through which the unity of the composition of the homogeneous manifold is thought in the concept of a **magnitude**, i.e., the appearances are all magnitudes, and indeed **extensive magnitudes**, since as intuitions in space or time they must be represented through the same synthesis as that through which space and time in general are determined.

This is not yet an explanation of how one can pick out apples against a background in ordinary perception. That explanation—whatever else it would require—would have to include Kant's arguments about the roles of the pure concepts of quality and substance in making experience possible. By means of pure concepts of quality, we become conscious of what is "real" in perception (again, color is an example), and by means of the pure concept of substance we become conscious of objects as things that retain their identities over time, even as they undergo changes. But we have seen this much: that in order to pick out objects as extended spatial things we must think them (implicitly) through the concept of magnitude. When you count up apples, one aspect of what makes them countable units is that each one *can be* encountered as a magnitude. The pure concept grounds and makes possible what happens in real empirical experience.

■

It might seem that we have completed our task. By this winding path we have come to see how to make good on Kant's claim that number is "a representation that summarizes the successive addition of one (homogeneous) unit to another." We have seen that even if, as Kant insists time and again, we must have something sensible at hand in order to count (e.g., fingers or dots on a page), the deep basis for such counting is the work of consciousness on the forms of intuition through pure concepts. We have also seen, on the one hand, that "summarizing" the process of counting is rooted ultimately in the pure synthetic unity of consciousness and, on the other hand, that counting must be temporally successive since the form of inner sense is time.

We have not, however, yet accounted for the necessity entailed in mathematical propositions. Our investigation thus far provides a way to understand what we are doing (both empirically and transcendentally) when we add 5 to 7. But how do we know we are doing it correctly? Where does the conviction that we are getting the right answer come from? This is our culminating question and takes us once more into some strange corners of Kant's text. (In the interest of not making our time with Kant overly long, the remainder of the chapter is considerably more compressed than what we have already been through. This is warranted to the extent that all of the basic concepts have been outlined. We still need to do some work with these concepts.)

IS IT CREDIBLE that magnitude (as the interplay of unity, plurality, and totality) is a pure concept? That is, can we accept Kant's claim that this concept has independence from intuition, from space and time? Doesn't the concept of a magnitude necessarily require either spatial or temporal extension?

If we insist on this feature of what magnitude means to us, Kant will meet us half way: pure concepts, as conditions for experience, have significance only in relation to intuitions. (Recall, "thoughts without content are empty.") Put somewhat differently, pure concepts only have objective import when making the objects of experience available for consciousness. On their own, pure concepts are only forms for thinking. No objects—even the objects of pure mathematics—can be thought by means of concepts alone.

We spent a lot of time considering what a pure form of intuition is. We can deal with the question of a pure form of thought more quickly. Consider again the concepts of unity, plurality, and totality. One mode of objective significance for these concepts, as we have seen, is to make possible the consciousness of counting. Counting the 23 apples in your basket requires thinking about the apples as units and the collection as both a plurality and a totality. These moments of thinking, however, can be mapped onto judgments such as "This is an apple," "Some of the things on the ground are apples," and "All the apples I have picked are in the basket." The forms of these judgments do not indicate any relation to intuition. Taken only as judgment forms, nothing is yet thought in "this," "some," and "all."[16] We can see again how experience itself remains the touchstone for Kant's thinking: pure forms of thought, while transcendentally necessary, have no significance—do nothing—outside of the role they play in making experience possible.

IF THE QUESTION hasn't occurred to you, Kant will raise it for you: how can pure intuition and pure concepts come together in the first place? Pure intuitions have nothing conceptual in them and pure concepts are in no way intuitive. That is, cognition is both receptive and spontaneous. But we saw above that ordinary perception is grounded in the consciousness of the unity of the manifold of intuition through the concept of magnitude. We did not stop to ask how these heterogeneous powers can be related to each other. As we will see, Kant's answer to this question holds the key to arithmetic necessity.

As Kant sees it, the difficulty is acute, but clear cut: on the one hand, a bridge must be built between intuition and thought, and that bridge must be homogeneous with intuition on one side and thought on the other; on the other hand, this bridge must somehow issue from our pure cognitive powers themselves. Kant calls the process of bridge building *schematism* and the bridge itself a *schema*. The account of the schematism is one of the most obscure in Kant's text; even he himself says that schematism is "a hidden art in the depths of the human soul." We will have to attempt some understanding of this obscure art since it turns out that at its deepest level, number itself is a schema.

We have been leaning on the phrase "a representation that summarizes the successive addition of one (homogeneous) unit to another" as Kant's understanding of number. The full sentence in which that phrase occurs reads:

> The pure **schema of magnitude** (*quantitatis*), however, as a concept of the understanding, is **number**, which is a representation that summarizes the successive addition of one (homogeneous) unit to another. (A142/B182)

We learned just above that as a pure concept magnitude does not relate to any intuition; it names certain forms of judgment. In our treatment of magnitude with respect to the perception of extended objects, we assumed straightaway that we could think the moments of unity, plurality, and totality in the extended thing. It turns out that number, as one instance of a "hidden art" at work in us, made this thinking about extended things possible.

TWO OF KANT'S own examples will help us understand what it means to call number a schema. He begins his discussion of schematism by noting that empirical concepts already contain a relation to intuition. Kant writes:

> [T]he empirical concept of a **plate** has homogeneity with the pure geometrical concept of a **circle**, for the roundness that is thought in the former can be intuited in the latter. (A137/B176)

When Kant says that roundness is thought in the concept of a plate, he must mean that roundness *as a concept* is included in the concept of a plate. It is one of the predicates that might be mentioned in explaining what a plate is. In this regard, roundness is part of a discursive treatment of plates. But without an intuitive grasp of roundness, the concept of roundness is empty. Neither "plate" nor "roundness" is a pure concept.

However, Kant suggests that our use of the concept of roundness makes contact with intuition through the "pure geometric concept of a circle." How and why is this the case? Kant explains this in a discussion of triangles. We will consider this discussion and then show that the same must be true of circles. Note at the outset that the phrase "pure geometric" indicates that our access to circles is somehow not dependent on experience (that's the pure part), but necessarily tied to intuition (since geometry is science of spatial magnitudes).

Kant writes:

> No image of a triangle would ever be adequate to the
> concept of it. For it would not attain the generality of
> the concept [i.e., three-sided rectilinear plane figure],
> which makes it valid for all triangles, right or acute,
> etc., but would always be limited to one part of this
> sphere. The schema of the triangle can never exist any-
> where except in thought, and signifies a rule of the
> synthesis of the imagination with regard to pure shapes
> in space. (A141/B180)

In one sense, it would suffice, if asked what a triangle is,
to give a discursive answer: "A triangle is a closed figure
bounded by three straight lines." One doesn't need to sup-
plement this with a drawing of such a figure. But if your
discursive answer is understood by the person asking, that
person will be able to produce the drawing. Why? Because
the real meaning of "triangle" is grounded neither in
words nor in an image, but in a rule for determining space.
Instead of a discursive definition, one might instead say:
"Draw a straight line. Then draw another one starting from
one endpoint of the first. Now draw a third straight line
between the other endpoints. If you do this, you will have
a triangle." Notice the overlap between this and the discursive definition: both are completely general; both have the
same elements (three lines, boundedness, etc.). Kant's suggestion seems to be that the meaning contained in the discursive definition is rooted in an implicit procedure that is
entailed in drawing a triangle. "Triangle" is not at bottom a
space determined in a certain way; it is a way of *determining*
space. Without the schema as a rule for determining space,
the concept of a triangle would be without significance. It
would be a concept without an object.

The same would be true of circles. A circle can be defined as a certain kind of determined space. In Euclid's definition, a circle is "a plane figure contained by one line such that all the straight lines falling upon it from one point among those lying within the figure equal one another." The schema of a circle, it seems, would be something like "draw a line by rotating a line segment around one of its endpoints." The roundness that we intuit in the image of a circle is grounded in the rule of its production.

THE ROUNDNESS THOUGHT in the concept of a plate makes contact with intuition through the concept of a circle; but the concept of a circle makes contact with intuition through the schema as rule for determining pure intuition. Plates can be perceived and circles can be drawn. How is it with numbers? How does number as a schema relate to intuition? To approach this question, we need to attend to a difference between numbers and geometric figures.

There is no image of triangles as such. Any image of a triangle must, for instance, be of either an acute, right, or obtuse triangle. The image cannot match the universality of the concept (while the schema can). In contrast, Kant writes that "if I place five points in a row, ... , this is an image of the number five" (A140/B179). The possibility of providing this image springs from the fact that individual numbers are singular in a way that triangles are not. There is only one 5, but innumerable unique triangles. Highlighting this difference, however, obscures the most important aspects of number.

First, it should be clear to us by now that the image provided by the dots *is not a number*. Without being counted up and held together in consciousness, there is no number of dots. Regarding the dots as an image of the number five presumes already what is involved in numerating them. Second, we noted long ago that even if 7 and 5 are unique numbers in one sense, in another sense they are found everywhere we count up items: seven apples here, five oranges there. We are still searching for what makes counting possible.

COUNTING IS A RULE, and numbers are made possible by this rule. More precisely, unique numbers are made possible by the rule that grounds number universally.

> [I]f I only think a number in general, which could be five or a hundred, this thinking is more the representation of a method for representing a multitude (e.g., a thousand) in accordance with a certain concept than the image itself . . . Now this representation of a general procedure of the imagination for providing a concept with its image is what I call the schema for this concept. (A140/B179–80)

We have seen how the last sentence pertains to triangles: the schema of a triangle as a rule for determining the form of outer sense (space) links the concept of a triangle with the possibility of producing an image.

For what concept is "number in general" as a "method for representing a multitude" the schema? We saw which above: *magnitude*. So we have finally reached the heart of the matter: How is magnitude as a pure concept brought into relation with intuition? And why is number the rule that makes this possible?

Time is the key to schematizing pure concepts. Recall that time is the form of order for all appearances since even outer intuitions must be brought to consciousness through the successive form of inner sense. Kant writes, "Time, as the formal condition of the manifold of inner sense, *thus of the connection of all representations*, contains an *a priori* manifold in pure intuition" (A138/B177) [my emphasis]. Also, "time is contained in every empirical representation of the manifold" (A139/B178). The unity of consciousness hinges on the unity of time as the form of order of all representations. Unity of a manifold is thought in terms of the interplay of unity, plurality, and totality. Number, as the schema of the concepts of magnitude, is the rule for unifying intuition as a moment of consciousness. *Consciousness of any manifold relies on the conceptual determination of inner sense.*

WE SEE ONLY NOW the full weight of calling number "a representation that summarizes the successive addition of one (homogeneous) unit to another." At bottom this is not about what 5 and 7 are. It is not even about the rule that makes it possible to count to 5 or 7. The ultimate significance of number is that it is the rule by which consciousness itself—as consciousness of a manifold—is made possible. *Without the successive gathering of representations into a whole, experience is not possible. Without the concepts of unity, plurality, and totality, this gathered whole can be nothing for consciousness.*

Number names the deepest activity that constitutes the unity of a mind both sensible and intelligible.

■

[E]ven the possibility of mathematics must be shown in transcendental philosophy (A733/B761).

Kant believes that the necessity we encounter in mathematical statements is unassailable. This necessity requires an explanation. We have found this explanation in the rules (schemata) by which mathematical concepts can determine our pure forms of intuition. Mathematics possesses necessity because it follows rules and because those rules give rise to objects. Without our ability to bring determination to our forms of intuition (resulting in "a product of the imagination" [A140/B179]), mathematical concepts would be empty thoughts.

But this explanation is not itself the business of mathematics. The principles of mathematical thought are the principles of possible experience. The investigation of these principles must be rooted in experience. Real experience remains always the touchstone for transcendental philosophy. The discernment of the minimal formal structure of experience in general differs fundamentally from mathematical thinking. And the establishment of the principles underlying that structure is entirely different from mathematical proof. Mathematics begins its work with definitions and proceeds to construct and manipulate its objects (thoughtfully) in pure intuition. Philosophical thought must endeavor to find the grounds of experience through "bare words," as Theodorus puts it *Theaetetus*. Yet bare words need not be mere chatter. Philosophical speech endeavors to light up what lies deepest in ordinary things.

THOUGHT/BEING

To unsettle.

THE PHILOSOPHER SAYS, "Thought and being are the same." Common sense finds this ridiculous. Indeed, ridicule seems to be the proper response to such grandiose nonsense. What could be plainer than that beings are *out there*, existing on their own, not at all dependent on my thoughts or anyone else's. Thoughts aren't out there, they're *in here*, in my head or yours. Beings are concrete. Thoughts are, as we say, only "mental." This seems to be proven to me at every turn in my dealings with the world. I have to accommodate my thoughts to the way things are. The world is a certain way. My task is to figure out how the world is. This figuring out is felt as an effort to bring my thoughts in line with the world. But even if some measure of correspondence is achieved, being and thought remain different in kind. Take my thoughts away and the world remains as it is. Being is essential; thought is not.

Bringing one's thoughts in line with beings we call knowing. You know this or that when your thoughts match this state of affairs or that one. As you pick apples in the orchard you know that the sun is shining because you see it in the sky; you know that the wind is blowing because you feel it on your skin; you know that the birds are chirping because you hear them in the trees. This kind of knowing comes easily. It only requires that you take in what is available to your senses. And such knowing is closest to the common-sense attitude described above. Knowing that the sun is shining, that the wind is blowing and that the birds are chirping adds nothing to these states of affairs. You simply register that these things are the case.

Such knowing, in fact, seems to be the very model for what common sense takes all knowing to be: copying what is within the mind. True knowledge begins here, with attentive registering within the mind what is out there.

The experience of knowing is not only taking in and aligning one's thoughts with what is, it is also to be certain of this taking in and aligning. Not only do you know that the sun is shining, you *know* that you know it. This second aspect of knowing may not be present to your mind when you take in the shining sun, but it is latent, secretly at work. If asked whether the sun is shining, you will say yes. This shows that seeing the sun is not just a matter of light hitting your eyes and triggering motions within your body. In answering yes you show that you are conscious of something.

Being ready to attest to knowing something includes being ready to say *how* you know it. "Is the sun shining?" "Yes." "How do you know?" "Because I see it, right up there in the sky." Someone might try to make trouble for you at this point—"But how do you *know* what you are seeing is really there?" You will have none of this—"I know the difference between really seeing something and imagining it. I see the sun shining *because* it is up there."

Notice the difference in the following scenario. You walk to work and on the way the sun is shining. You are now in a windowless conference room and a colleague asks, "Is it sunny outside?" You say, "I *think* so. It was sunny when I walked here earlier. But I'm not sure if it is now." Your colleague says, "I guess I'll know when I get back to my office." (Your colleague, of course, has an office with a window.)

Common sense asserts that what is the case *here* and *now* is the basis for knowing. Knowledge is attainable *there*, but only if you are there and not here. Knowledge *was* attainable earlier, but is no longer. Knowledge *will be* attainable later, but not yet. Knowing is rooted in the here and now. Because *this* is *here* and *now*, you can know.

IT TURNS OUT that common sense is philosophical after all. It has a theory of knowledge. Not only does it have such a theory, it implicitly appeals to that theory during its episodes of knowing—it knows why it knows what it knows.

Our question now is this: Is the common-sense attitude about experience consistent with its implicit theory? Let's linger over the features of this attitude before putting it to the test. As noted above, common sense sees experience (and the knowledge attained in experience) as receptive. One need only take in what is available in sensation to gain knowledge. Furthermore, common sense regards these acts of reception to yield *true* knowledge. Another feature should be added to this sketch, for common sense also regards its (apparently) immediately receptive knowledge as the fullest, most vibrant kind of knowledge. Our testing of the theory of common sense will attempt to verify these three features: immediate receptivity, truth, and maximum fullness and vibrancy.

HOW CAN WE go about conducting such a test? We will start with two questions. What kind of things are those which common sense regards as the basis of knowledge? How does common sense talk about these things?

Common sense says that knowledge is grounded in the presence of *this* thing *here* and *now*. Which this? The sunshine or the chirping birds? Which here? The orchard full of sunshine and chirping birds? Was not your bedroom *here* when you awoke on the day of apple picking? And which *now*? The now of arriving at the orchard? Isn't that now a *then*, now that you are nearly finished picking apples?

Common sense will understand the force of these questions. Indeed, it will agree that everything is a this. Everywhere is a here. Every moment of time is a now. Will common sense go along, however, when we insist that since everything is a this, "this" names nothing in particular? That since everywhere is a here, "here" names no particular place? That since every moment of time is a now, "now" names no particular moment of time?

It might. But common sense will likely go further and say, "When I said *this* was the basis of my knowing I didn't mean just any this, I meant this *tree*." Has common sense helped itself here? What is meant by "this tree"? We stand in an apple orchard filled with trees. Is not every tree entitled to the designation "this tree"? Well, "No," says common sense. "I do not mean just any one of these trees by 'this tree.' I mean *this* one"—and it points to a tree.

Common sense says, "*This* tree" and points. It says something general, but means something particular. Common sense regroups. "When I say 'this tree here,' I mean this one that I am looking at, pointing to right now. That is the one that I know about right now." If we continue to point out that common sense has said nothing new, that what it says still can apply to any tree anywhere, it will say—what? Something like, "But it is not *any* tree *anywhere* that I mean to name, but *this one right here!*" And then it will throw up its arms.

Should any of this bother us? Common sense will shake this off and say, "Sure. Words are general. Words can always be applied to more than one thing. But my experience is not of words. My experience is of what I see, and hear, and feel. *That* is the real content of experience and knowledge."

What might bother *us* is that common sense seems to have shifted its understanding of what knowing is. Common sense said that knowing was a receiving of a *this*, *here* and *now*. Two difficulties emerged. On the one hand, thises, heres, and nows seem not to be the kind of stable things that could ground knowing: this becomes that; here moves over there; now is always becoming then. On the other hand, when common sense attempted to *say* what it knew immediately through being receptive, it could not say what it meant. It said, "This thing here," but meant . . . Well, saying what it meant still eludes us. Instead of saying, common sense resorted to pointing. "When I said I had knowledge of this thing here, I meant *that*." [Cue pointing.]

It is not clear that common sense needs to move past pointing. It might be satisfied with this. But if it is bothered by its inability to say what it means, it might venture the alternative that was broached above. The shift is subtle. The content of knowledge remains the same—shining sun, chirping birds, blowing wind—but the basis for counting as knowledge has been displaced. What really counts now is that *I* see the shining, *I* hear the chirping, *I* feel the blowing. *I* am the ground of knowing.

But common sense will get nowhere with this shift. Here and now I see the shining sun, hear the chirping birds, and feel the blowing wind. But earlier I saw my bedroom, heard the alarm clock, and felt the cold floor. If *I* am to be the ground of knowing through seeing or hearing or feeling, do *I* remain the same when I see, hear, or feel different things? *I* seem to be like *this*, *here*, and *now*, something completely general, nothing in particular. Likewise, common sense says, "*I* contain a wealth of sensory knowledge," but everyone is "I." What common sense says of itself cannot distinguish it from any other I that says it knows something. When common sense says "I," it means something that eludes what is said.[1]

WHAT DOES common sense mean when it says that sensory knowledge is true knowledge? Truth here means that the "mental" content matches or copies what is out there. Common sense believes that its experience confirms this matching of thought and being. But as noted at the outset, for common sense this matching places all real weight on being. The things out there make it possible for me to have (sensory) knowledge. But we see here that the conviction of common sense that its sensory knowledge is immediate and unlimitedly rich are of a piece with its understanding of truth. The truth of sensory knowledge is grounded in the purported immediate receptivity of beings. And the supposed infinite variety of beings grounds the unlimited richness of this immediate knowing. These three features of the common-sense attitude about knowing stand or fall together.

There is no denying that common sense is *certain* that it has true, immediate, and infinitely rich knowledge through sensation. It will do no good to suggest that common sense goes wrong in this feeling of certainty. Standing in the apple orchard on a sunny day certainly is different from standing there on a rainy one. The question we must ask is whether a feeling of certainty can be equated with possessing truth. When we ask this question, we do not ask it from the perspective of common sense. Common sense as such cannot be shaken from its belief that certainty is the marker of truth.

Do we have reason to doubt what common sense believes? If so, it cannot be a doubt that common sense believes what it believes, but whether it should believe it. And this places the crux of the matter on what common sense—when pressed—says is the basis for its belief in immediate, rich, and true knowledge. That is, we need to look again at common sense's own reasons for believing what it believes.

But immediately we run into a problem. Common sense seemed to have two ways of indicating its reasons for taking certainty as truth. At first it said that *this here now* was the basis of its knowledge. When this way of speaking came up short, common sense resorted to pointing. Pointing at something was for common sense a way of explaining. Let's consider this second attempt first.

We ask common sense how it knows what it knows and it points at something. Perhaps pointing can sometimes be an adequate way to answer a question. Someone asks, "Which apple would you like?," and you point to one. No words seem needed to answer this question. Why? Because the question itself asks for a particular thing as an answer. Likewise, if we asked common sense about the basis of what it knows at just this moment, perhaps it would suffice for it to point at something. But this has not been our question. We have not sought an explanation of what is making some particular knowledge possible at some particular moment, but rather an answer in principle about what makes knowing possible *at all*. Pointing cannot answer such a question.

The first attempt made by common sense to answer the question was better, at least in this respect: it gave a general answer to a general question. "Because there are things here and there, now and then, knowing is possible." The form of the answer fits the question. But our question, again, is whether this answer gets to the truth of the matter. We are ready now to say that this account cannot be the true one. Why? What's wrong with this answer? Common sense is certain that what it knows matches the beings that make this knowing possible. Such knowing is a particular episode of knowing, with particular content. But the purportedly true explanation of this episode does not match the content.

MAYBE, THOUGH, the problem is with us. Maybe we shouldn't be asking these questions. Maybe the questions themselves create the illusion of a problem about giving a true explanation of knowing. Perhaps the feeling of certainty in sensory knowing is beyond questioning. Some reflection shows that this cannot be the case. If we were correct at the outset to assert that—even for common sense—knowing is accompanied by a knowing that I know and by an implicit understanding of what makes my knowing possible, then our questioning is only a way of exposing the contradiction inherent in common sense.

Why contradiction? Because the certainty that common sense possesses is the opposite of what it seems. Common sense regards its certainty as an immediate effect of its reception of beings. It appears to us now, however, that this certainty is mediated by common sense's own (implicit) theory of knowing. As a knower, common sense does not regard itself as simply a mirror that reflects beings. In addition, common sense has not appeared to us as simply passive. Common sense always has some regard for itself in its knowing. And this self-regard is rooted in its possession of an always-ready answer to the very question we have posed: how does it know what it knows? Certainty does not come directly and immediately from beings. The certainty of common sense that it possesses true knowledge of *this here now* must pass through its conviction that *this here now* is the basis for what it knows. Immediate knowing turns out to be mediated knowing.

Common sense grounds its certainty of particulars through thoughts framed around universals (*this here now*). At this point, we might note that with the recognition that mediation is present in common sense it is now possible to construe common sense not as power of receiving and registering external things, but as a cast of mind that contains certain presuppositions. Common sense, by means of its presupposed guideposts, is a way of being oriented in the world. Common sense makes sense of its awareness of worldly things through this framework. Regarding common sense in this way will help to see further how its certainty fails to attain truth.

Once again, common sense is certain, at any particular moment in any particular place, of a particular state of affairs. It takes the content of this certainty as true knowledge. But it has already said to itself—as it were—that all episodes of certainty are grounded in *this here now*. So when we say that common sense cannot claim to have attained truth in its certainty it is because the *terms* of its grounding do not match the content of its certainty. Common sense regards knowledge as being conferred by particulars, but it justifies its claims of knowing in terms of universals. The truth of all knowing for common sense is *this here now*.

But this must surely be wrong. Can there be any doubt

that when you see the green leaves of the trees in the orchard that you are not only certain of seeing green leaves but that it is true that the leaves are green? Are we really to think that when you feel the bark on the tree, you are not feeling its rough texture but only a *this*? Peeling these questions apart will show more fully in what way common sense cannot call its certainty truth. We will also be able finally to see how—despite its belief otherwise—the knowledge possessed by common sense is in fact the emptiest, not the fullest, kind of knowing.

The first thing to note is that the terms in which these questions are asked already exceed the frame of mind that we have been calling common sense. When the truth of apparently immediate sensory knowledge is threatened to be reduced to the most general of universals, common sense shifts its framework. Instead of claiming to be in touch with a particular *this*, common sense now says it is making contact with colors and textures. In an attempt to confer truth on its certainty, it abandons the view that *this here now* is the basis for knowing and replaces it with a different view. The new view is that sensory knowledge makes contact with the *properties* of objects. Common sense now asserts that we come to know things *through* their properties.

This shifting of views is an easy one for common sense. In fact, it will say that this is what it had in mind all along, for what is more commonplace than to know that seeing must be a seeing of colors, and touch a feeling of texture, and so on for our other senses. Sensory knowledge is knowledge of sense qualities. We need not continue to interrogate common sense to see some implications of this seemingly reasonable reorientation. First, in making this move, common sense itself will have acknowledged that immediate knowledge of particulars is not possible. For if

we know things through their properties, then we do not
know them immediately. All knowledge of objects will be
mediated.[2] Second, common sense itself will have shown
us the clearest way in which its former views cannot ground
true knowledge, for it turns out (under its new view) that
true knowledge is not of particulars as particulars, but of
particulars as possessors of sensible qualities. If the truth of
my sensory knowledge in the apple orchard is grounded
in the fact that seeing green matches the being green of
the leaves, then it cannot be true that I know about something like a leaf simply as a *this*. At this point we can frame
a rather disorienting sentence: Common sense—and don't
we all have this sense—is certain that it can know all about
things because they are here and now, but this is not true.

■

If common sense is philosophical—philosophical because
it thinks about its awareness of beings—it doesn't know it.
The root of the difficulties that common sense has in articulating the basis of its knowing and the contradictions inherent in its understanding of its own experience is that it fails
to acknowledge that it thinks in this way. Common sense
seems to take its understanding of how knowing is possible
as itself a product of immediacy and receptivity, that its way
of understanding things comes to it directly from things. It
seemed to us that common sense, rather, approached beings
with this understanding already in hand. This is what we
meant in saying that its certainty is mediated by its understanding of how knowledge is possible.

This feature of consciousness is retained even as common sense reforms its understanding of knowing. When
common sense says that knowledge of beings is obtained
through the apprehension of their properties, we can see

that common sense is again a more sophisticated thinker than it will acknowledge. When consciousness sees its awareness of beings through this lens, it seems obvious to consciousness that *there just are* things possessing properties. But we could submit this reformed version of common sense to another round of questioning and expose again both its contradictoriness and the way that its thoughts mediate what appears to consciousness as immediate. Consider only these questions: If a "thing" is known through its many properties, how do we know there is a thing there at all? If knowledge is now seen as grounded in the immediate apprehension of properties, won't the world of things dissolve into a stew of free-floating properties? "Thing" seems to be a product of consciousness and not something directly encountered in the world.

Common sense isn't used to thinking about such things, but at some point it might occur to it—and this is yet another mode of common sense—that it has a better answer to the question about knowing. The better answer is that true knowledge comes neither through direct contact with things nor by means of perceiving sense qualities, but rather through scientific investigation. The *true beings* behind what is available to common experience are the objects of scientific study. Real knowledge—it turns out—is not a knowing of simple *thises* or of things through their properties, but knowledge of the hidden principles at work in the objects of ordinary sense experience.

Common sense finds itself in an awkward position at this point. It is a common opinion that science gets at what is really true in things and therefore is knowing *par excellence*. But it is also a common opinion that this knowledge is not available to everyone—at least not without a great deal of work and study. Hence this common opinion is only an opinion. This mode of common sense believes that science provides true knowledge without necessarily having an experience of such knowing.

Therefore, if we want to scrutinize this claim about scientific knowledge we have to leave common sense behind and take up scientific consciousness itself as our object.

The paradigm of scientific knowing for common sense is mathematical physics and the paradigm of mathematical physics is Isaac Newton's *Principia*. The "discovery"[3] of gravity that Newton accomplishes in this work stands for common opinion as the very model of scientific knowledge. Newton's work will serve us well for it provides both a clear-cut example of where science and common sense meet and a fully worked out instance of scientific explanation.

Science and common sense meet since both hold that knowing is grounded in what is *out there*. Common sense supposed that knowing is made possible either by *thises* or by sense qualities. Science is motivated by the supposition that hidden things—causes—explain ordinary phenomena. To know about these hidden things is to really know what is true in things.

This is why the single word "gravity" has such purchase on ordinary consciousness. The word itself carries the promise of true knowing because although we cannot see gravity itself, we can "know" that it is the secret engine at work behind the scenes.

It is no accident that Newton's "universal gravitation" is called a *force*. We will do well to contemplate the basic move to force as the ground of knowing, in advance of a close look at Newton's work.

If we had pursued further the questions prompted by the notion of a *thing with properties*, we would have found ourselves with insuperable difficulties. We have encountered these difficulties already with Aristotle, the central node of which is the problem of how to bring together *many* properties in *one* thing. The question is always, "What is the source of oneness in a thing that possesses a multitude of properties or qualities?" As long as the properties themselves are taken to be thing-like themselves—independent and *out there*—the unity of objects cannot be comprehended.

The move to forces solves the problem. How? First we must see that "force" here is just a stand-in for a *something* that would explain things in a certain way. The explanation would go like this: Ordinary objects of sensory experience are not bundles of free-floating properties—rather both things and their properties are nothing but a play of forces—the forces are *in themselves one thing*, but manifest themselves to our senses in multiple ways. The color of salt is not something different from its shape or taste in the salt itself. Salt, as a certain play of forces, is one thing. But this one thing can express itself variously. The multiplicity of properties is an external show of what is inwardly unitary.

Said this way, one has not yet said *what* these forces are; but one has laid out a picture of what knowledge of salt would be: knowing what those forces are.

Our task ahead will divide into two parts. On the one hand, we will have to unfold the layers of this general view of knowing—what are its presuppositions and are they coherent? On the other hand, we will have to ask whether the expectation of scientific consciousness can be fulfilled—can we know about a force as a simple something that exists out in the world? While a close look at some aspects of Newton's *Principia* will allow us to approach the second question, the first can be taken up provisionally independently of Newton's book.

THE VIEW THAT the world is a play of forces and that knowledge of the world is knowledge of these forces is organized around the distinction between the world as it is inwardly for itself—the forces themselves—and the external show of these forces—the world as it is for us. This distinction has two far-reaching consequences.

The world as apprehended by the senses is now (at least implicitly) seen as the *appearance* of the world. What is the difference between appearance thus construed and the sensory world of common sense? In its prior modes, common sense had no notion of something standing behind what is apprehended in sensory episodes. The *this* or sense qualities were apprehended directly. The true objects of knowledge were not hidden from sensory apprehension. But when the sensory world *as* sensory is taken as an outward expression or show of something inward, consciousness will have come to regard itself as cut off from the truth of things if only the sensory is considered. But since the sensory world is regarded as the appearing of the true being of things, consciousness will not take itself to be cut off from the truth of things if it can get behind this veil of appearances. Let us recognize that this is a rather sophisticated notion: appearance as the showing of something that in itself remains hidden from view.

In addition, since force, as the true inward being of things, is not in itself available to sensation, it must be an object for the intellect. This is, in a way, only a corollary of the notion of appearance. If the outward show of forces is not what forces are in themselves, then forces cannot be known *as* sensory things.

This, however, turns out to be a point of great tension for the scientific view of the world. Why? Because the scientific view, as we noted, shares with common sense the opinion that there is something *out there*—something real and substantial, not something thought—that is the ground of knowing. For scientific consciousness the effort of thought that is involved in getting at the invisible causes behind visible phenomena is regarded as inessential. Like common sense, scientific consciousness says that the true is wholly on the side of being. We will have to see if this position can be maintained.

That this picture of a world underpinned by forces is shared by Newton can be readily gleaned from his preface to the *Principia*.[4] He writes that "the basic problem of philosophy [i.e., "natural philosophy" or, as we would say, science] seems to be to discover the forces of nature from the phenomena" (382). The full scope of Newton's book takes in "gravity, levity, elastic forces, resistance of fluids, and forces of this sort, whether attractive or impulsive." Newton frames his project by analogy with the study of machines, in particular the question of how much force is needed to move a given object with a given machine. Forces pertain most especially to the movement of bodies.

The central problem of Newton's book is to "derive from celestial phenomena the gravitational forces by which bodies tend toward the sun and toward the individual planets" (382). We will attempt to comprehend the manner of explanation that Newton employs in establishing that it is one and the same force—gravity—that is responsible for the motions of the planets around the sun and the moons around their planets as it is for ordinary bodies to fall to the earth. The establishment of gravity as a *universal* attraction of all bodies to each other will stand for us as an example of the general picture sketched above: many disparate phenomena will be traced back to one indwelling force. We can frame our central question about this establishment of

a unitary force with the same terms that we used in scrutinizing common sense: Is scientific consciousness' *certainty*
that gravity in itself is the cause of phenomena an attaining of *truth*?

While the derivation of universal gravitation from phenomena will be our focus, it is worth noting further the
extent to which Newton shares, in principle, the view that
the world is ultimately a play of forces. After outlining the
scope of investigation carried out in the *Principia*, Newton
writes,

> If only we could derive the other phenomena of nature
> from mechanical principles by the same kind of rea-
> soning! For many things lead me to have a suspicion
> that all phenomena may depend on certain forces by
> which particles of bodies, by causes not yet known,
> either are impelled toward one another and cohere in
> regular figures, or are repelled from one another and
> recede. Since these forces are unknown, philosophers
> have hitherto made trial of nature in vain. (382–3)

Our study of Newton's work on gravity is meant to illustrate something about this more general view about what is
true in world.

UNIVERSAL GRAVITATION cannot be deduced from
direct observation—not even from a generalizing of many
observations. While careful observation (i.e., measurement)
of certain visible phenomena (e.g., the rate at which bodies
fall near the earth and the diameters and periodic times of
the orbits of celestial bodies) is indispensable, it cannot on
its own establish the existence of a unitary force. Observation must be coupled with a theoretical study of bodies moving under forces. Newton calls this kind of study

"rational mechanics," that is, "the science, expressed in exact proportions and demonstrations, of the motions that result from any forces whatever and of the forces that are required for any motions whatever" (382).

The project of the first two books of the *Principia*, then, is not to discern how any particular, really-encountered bodies in the world are moving and by what forces; it is rather to explore in principle how bodies *would move* when subjected to certain forces and *which forces* would be responsible for certain kinds of movement.

But to undertake such a project—one that endeavors to establish what would happen in principle—requires first establishing principles. We will not attempt to probe what might be entailed in and questionable about the establishment of principles of motion. We will only note that Newton begins the *Principia* in the way that mathematicians begin their treatises—with a set of definitions. The subject matter of these definitions are matter, motion, and force. But the focus of the definitions is mathematical. We find definitions of "*quantity* of matter" and "*quantity* of motion," for instance. (Matter and motion themselves are not defined.) The "inherent force of matter" is also framed essentially in a mathematical way, since it is said to be "proportional to the [quantity of matter in a] body" (404). Definitions 6, 7, and 8 specify certain quantities of centripetal force.

Only definitions 4 and 5 are not immediately mathematical in character. These are the definitions of impressed force and centripetal force, respectively. A glance at these definitions will, nevertheless, show that Newton's "rational mechanics" must be a thoroughly mathematical affair.

Impressed force is defined as "the action exerted on a body to change its state either of resting or of moving uniformly straight forward" (i.e., in a straight line at a constant velocity). This means that if a body moves along a curved path, impressed forces must be responsible for this curvy motion. Let us note that "action" here is a kind of place-holder at best, and a red herring at worst. Newton's *Principia* will not endeavor to reveal the nature of such actions. All that rational mechanics can establish is *how much* "action" is involved in determining a given motion. Rational mechanics cannot investigate how a force changes the motion of a body, it can only study the amount of force that corresponds to a given change of motion.[5]

Centripetal force is defined as a kind of impressed force. But again, kind here is limited to a mathematical discrimination. Centripetal force is any impressed force *directed toward a center.* As a species of impressed force, centripetal force is marked out by its spatial—geometrical—character.

A REMARK MADE in his commentary on the definition of centripetal force requires our attention. If we fail to grasp its import, we cannot comprehend either the nature of Newton's accomplishment or the structure of scientific rationality.

Immediately following the definition of centripetal force, Newton writes, "One force of this kind is gravity, by which bodies tend toward the center of the earth" (405). This could seem a very strange statement given that the central aim of Newton's whole book seems to be to establish that gravity *is* the force that accounts for bodies "tending toward" the earth. Our misunderstanding would arise from taking Newton's reference to "gravity" in its post-Newtonian meaning, that is, in taking it to refer to a *universal force* at work in the cosmos. Newton does not mean it in this way, for "gravity" here refers only to what everyone always already knows: that bodies are heavy, hard to lift *away* from the earth. (The *Principia* is written in Latin, and "gravity" translates *gravitas*, which means simply heaviness or weight.) "Gravity" as the name of a force refers, at first, only to whatever is responsible for the heaviness of objects near the earth.

The fundamental move of Newton's inquiry, then, will be establishing that the force responsible for ordinary heaviness is the same force that is responsible for a variety of other phenomena. A useful image captures this move: it will be shown that the falling of a body *in a straight line* toward the earth is the same as the revolution *in a closed curve* of the moon around the earth.

Newton's "discovery" of gravity is not the discovery that a there is a force that attracts bodies to the earth. It is the determination that the attraction of bodies to the earth is just one manifestation of a force at work everywhere.[6]

IF RATIONAL MECHANICS cannot discern the nature of the "action" that causes a body to change its motion, what does it mean to say that rational mechanics studies "the motions that result from any forces whatever and of the forces that are required for any motions whatever"? Two examples will suffice to answer this question.

In the second proposition of the *Principia*, Newton proves[7] that a body that traces out equal areas in equal times (with respect to areas bounded by radii drawn to the center of force) is subject to a centripetal force. The proof makes no mention of how the force acts on the body. The only relevant characteristic of the force at issue is that it be directed toward some fixed point. Hence the proof shows that a particular kind of force (a centripetal one) is "required for" a certain kind of motion (one that traces equal areas in equal times). We see here an example of what was anticipated above: Newton's science of motions subject to forces is limited to the mathematical features of motions and forces.

In the fourth proposition, Newton considers the comparison of forces acting on multiple bodies that move uniformly (i.e., with constant velocities) in circles around the same center. It is proved in general that the forces acting on such bodies will be directed toward the same center. The sixth corollary to this proposition—which turns out to be an especially relevant case, as we will see—shows that if the times taken by the bodies to revolve around their common center are as the ³⁄₂ powers of their respective radii[8] then the amount of force acting on the bodies will vary inversely as the squares of the distances of the bodies from the center. The precise mathematical features of this claim need not slow us down, since the import for us is more general. As with the second proposition, this one establishes a relationship between a kind of force—one that varies as the square of distance—and a kind of motion—one that maintains a certain ratio.

All of rational mechanics proceeds in this way, regardless of how complicated its propositions become: different species of motions and forces are proven to "result from" or be "required for" each other, where the species are discriminated by mathematical differences.[9]

JOHANNES KEPLER had already shown, more than fifty years before the publication of the *Principia*, that the solar planets sweep out equal areas in equal times and that their periodic times are as the ³⁄₂ powers of their radii. These are known as Kepler's second and third laws, respectively.[10] Subsequent observations (using a variety of methods) established that the moons of Jupiter and Saturn—whose orbits "do not differ sensibly from circles" (797) and whose motions are uniform—also obey the ³⁄₂ power law.

These are not propositions of rational mechanics. That is, these are not claims about how a body would move subject to a certain kind of force or what force is required for a certain kind of motion. These are, as Newton calls them, *phenomena*. Note that one need not mention force at all to describe—as a matter of empirical observation[11]—how the planets and moons move. The very power of Newton's argument—and all science that proceeds in this way—relies on this.

Because he has already established in principle certain relationships between particular forces and particular motions, Newton can begin to determine the (mathematical character of) forces at work in the heavens. It will help to recapitulate some points made above before following the steps of this reasoning.

First, we must recall that the very framework of Newton's study of bodies in motion presupposes that forces are required to move bodies along curved paths. Inasmuch as celestial bodies have curved orbits, there must be forces acting upon them. Second, in his second and fourth propositions, Newton is able to show, on the one hand, that all bodies that follow Kepler's second law are subject to centripetal forces, and, on the other hand, that the forces acting on bodies following Kepler's third law will vary as the squares of the distances from the center of force.

The next move is straightforward: we must bring the results of rational mechanics to bear on our observations. Because the solar planets and the moons of Jupiter and Saturn describe certain motions, we can infer that the forces acting on them are of a certain sort. Because the moons of Jupiter and Saturn move uniformly in circles around their centers, we can infer that they are acted on by forces directed toward those centers. Because the solar planets sweep out equal areas in equal times, it can also be inferred that they are acted on by a force directed toward their common center. And because the bodies in each group (with respect to the other bodies in that group) obey the ³⁄₂ powers law, we can infer that the forces in each case vary as the squares of the distances from the centers.

It is important to see the limits of what has been established at this point. The sun and its planets, Jupiter and its moons, and Saturn and its moons, are all taken separately as discrete systems of bodies in motion. In each case, it can be inferred, by bringing the results of rational mechanics to bear on observed facts, that there is a centripetal force at work that varies as the square of distances. No claim has yet been made about how these systems of bodies might be related to each other or about how the forces present in each system are themselves related.

YET A DECISIVE STEP has been taken. We have asserted that forces *of a certain kind* are really at work in the heavens. The pivotal move is made when Newton brings the investigation down to earth. From the earth we will be able to reach back out to the heavens and tie the cosmos together.

Recall that at first "gravity" is limited to earthbound phenomena. Objects near the earth are heavy, they "tend" toward the earth. Within the framework of Newton's project, this tending must be caused by a force. Proposition 4 of Book III of the *Principia* asserts that the "moon gravitates toward the earth" (803). If this can be established, it will connect phenomena that we see and feel nearby—the falling of objects and their weights—with something remote and cut off from immediate experience. The argument backing up this claim could not be more elegant.

Once more, within the framework of rational mechanics bodies will travel in straight lines if not acted on by impressed forces. The moon does not move in a straight line—it follows a curve around the earth. This curvy motion must be the result of an impressed force acting on the moon. (And a smooth curve implies a continually acting force.) The mathematical techniques of rational mechanics allow us to decompose the curved motion of the moon into the straight-line motion that it would follow if not acted on by a force and the amount of deviation from that straight line in a given time. Once Newton determines, in Proposition 3, that the moon is subject to a centripetal force toward the center of the earth, he can calculate how much the moon would "fall" in a given time toward the earth if the moon were "deprived of all its motion" (its sideways motion, as it were). Newton's calculations determine that the moon falls 16 feet toward the earth every minute.[12] Newton also establishes in Proposition 3 that the centripetal force acting on the moon diminishes as the squares of distances.[13] Since the moon's orbit has a radius of 60 earth radii, the strength of the force that acts on the moon would be increased by 60×60 times at the surface of the earth. A force of this strength would cause a body to fall (starting from rest) 16 feet in *one second*.[14] And this is in fact the rate at which bodies fall near the earth!

Newton exploits this coincidence of mathematical determinations to assert that the force that keeps the moon in its orbit is *nothing but ordinary gravity*. Why, Newton asks, should we think that there are two different forces at work when the numbers allow us to attribute both the falling of objects near the earth and the revolution of the moon to the same force? At the beginning of Book III of the *Principia* Newton lays down "rules for the study of natural philosophy" (794) that include a rule that we should admit no more causes than are needed to explain phenomena and another that the same cause should be attributed to "effects of the same kind." Once Newton has analyzed the motion of the moon into one with a "falling" component, and shown that the rate of its falling is consistent with the rate at which bodies fall near the earth (given a variation of force as the squares of distances), attributing the force acting on the moon to something other than gravity would run afoul of these rules. *Ordinary gravity will now suffice to explain the orbital motion of the moon.* Indeed, if the force acting on the moon were something different than gravity, but nevertheless increased in strength 60×60 times at the surface of the earth, "then bodies making for the earth by both forces [i.e., "moon force" and ordinary gravity] acting together would descend twice as fast" and this is "entirely contrary to experience" (804).

THE FLOODGATES are now open. Since the motions of the solar planets and the moons of Jupiter and Saturn are "phenomena of the same kind as the revolution of the moon about the earth"—that is, have the same mathematical characteristics—we should attribute their motions to the same cause: *gravity*. Gravity is now understood to be at work in places far remote from the earth.

But even this move falls short of universal gravitation. All that has been said is that there is a force that moves certain bodies *toward* the center of the earth and that the same force directs other bodies (moons and planets) toward other centers (the centers of the sun, Jupiter and Saturn).

In Proposition 6 of Book III, Newton is able to establish—in ways similar to what we have already seen—that "*all bodies* gravitate toward each of the planets" (806). This claim finally removes the barriers between the different systems of celestial bodies upon which the argument has been relying and unites them into one system of moving bodies. This unification is achieved through the attribution of a common force acting across the different systems.

But Newton also establishes in Proposition 6 that the amount of force by which any body "gravitates" toward "any one planet" is proportional to the "quantity of matter which the body contains." It is with this claim that the final domino will fall. For Newton is able to generalize the picture in Proposition 7: "*Gravity exists in all bodies universally and is proportional to the quantity of matter in each*" (810).

∎

Scientific consciousness begins with the conviction that hidden forces are at work behind phenomena. The work of science is to look behind appearances to discern the causes underneath. Like the convictions of common sense, this conviction of scientific consciousness about forces grounds an understanding of what the true objects of knowledge are and what makes knowledge possible. We saw that what common sense pointed to as the ground of knowing turned out not to match what it believed was the nature of its knowledge. How is it with science? Does its actual experience of knowing match its conviction about what grounds knowing?

Newton certainly provides us with something impressive. The analytical power of rational mechanics coupled with the ingenuity that yields precise measurements of celestial motions allows us to comprehend a vast diversity of motions in the cosmos as all one kind of motion. The outward show of falling bodies and revolving planets and moons is but the *appearing* of a unitary indwelling force. Behind the flux of bodies undergoing unceasing change is a law of force that is unchanging. Despite the outward flux, the world can be understood as inwardly stable.

Consider how far-reaching the assertion of Proposition 7 is. When Newton is able to conclude that all bodies—and every part of a body is itself a body—have gravity, our understanding of gravity must undergo a qualitative shift. Even in the enunciation of Proposition 7 gravity is still spoken of as "existing in" bodies. This way of speaking doesn't ultimately fit with Newton's view of the world, since a body left to itself does not "tend" toward another body in the way that heavy bodies do. Indeed, it is one of the principles of rational mechanics that a force must be impressed to cause a body to be heavy. But this means that to say that "gravity exists in all bodies" is to say that all bodies are tending toward one another. This is where the notion of a universal *attraction* comes in. That all bodies tend toward one another must, within the framework of rational mechanics, be attributed to some "action" (call it attraction). As mutual attraction, gravity must be understood as a relationship between bodies, and not as something that each body possesses taken one by one. And since this mutual attraction—insofar as Newtonian science can grasp it—is determined by the distance between bodies and the quantity of matter in the bodies involved, the disposition of all bodies in the cosmos in relation to one another can be captured by one law.[15]

Consider further how outward complexity is compatible with—even necessitated by—inward simplicity. Proposition 11 of Book I of the *Principia* shows that the shape of a closed orbit of a body subject to a centripetal force that varies as the squares of distances must be an ellipse. And this is consistent with established observations of celestial bodies. Close scrutiny of planetary orbits, however, shows that they are not precisely elliptical. They deviate here and there, and the deviations themselves appear to vary from one revolution to the next. Scrutinized in this fine-grained way, the system of solar planets starts to look messy and imperfect. But this is wrong and Proposition 7 tells us why. Since all bodies are attracted to each other—that is, set each other in motion—we should not expect these bodies to trace out perfect ellipses. For instance, as Saturn and Jupiter happen to come nearer to each other in their revolutions around the sun, they tug more and more strongly on each other. This causes them to deviate from the ellipse each would follow if either could be alone with the sun in the cosmos. But even to see their influence on each other as a deviation from elliptical order is to miss the real principle of order and uniformity at work in their motions: *the law of gravitational force itself.* The whole apparently messy network of moving bodies in the cosmos is nothing but the lawful aggregate of all bodies pulling on—that is, falling toward—each other.

How can this not be true? The explanatory power of Newton's conclusion seems unimpeachable. As we will see, the failure of scientific consciousness to raise its certainty to truth is not a matter of being insufficiently explanatory.[16] The question is whether scientific consciousness has remained true to the picture of the world and knowing that motivated it to make the move to forces in the first place.

The notion of force was meant to deal with a problem that common sense could not solve, namely, the way in which the multiplicity of sense qualities could be understood to inhere in one thing. The proposed solution was simple: things are inwardly one, but outwardly many. *For us* salt appears square in shape, white to the eye and salty to the tongue, but is—so it was proposed—*in itself* one play of forces. The question for scientific consciousness is whether it can see through the outward show to discern the underlying forces *as something separate from phenomena and consciousness*. As with common sense, if scientific consciousness cannot make good on forces as a kind of essential being bearing the full weight of knowledge, then the view of the world as a play of forces cannot be regarded as true.

Our sketch of Newton's derivation of universal gravitation from phenomena is meant to stand in for this general mode of thought. The diversity of appearances it considers—falling bodies near the earth and the revolutions of planets and moons remote from the earth—are like the shape, color, and taste of salt: an outward show. Universal gravitation is the underlying unitary force of which this show would be the expression. Once again, the question for us is whether it is right to call universal gravitation what is *true* in the appearances.

Newton says that the goal of science "seems to be to discover the forces of nature from the phenomena." The phenomena show themselves to us, and they show themselves as diverse and ever-changing. To *understand* them would be to discern something unitary and unchanging within.

A diversity of ever-changing free motions are visible in the cosmos. But can universal gravitation be understood as something apart from these motions? Is the idea of a true inward world that shows itself in an apparent one consistent with the notion of universal gravitation? It is not. Why?

The crux of the issue has to do with the relationship between force and motion. The framework of rational mechanics posits that impressed forces are the *cause* of deviations from uniform straight-line motions. But has this framework really made intelligible *what* a force is such that it can be this kind of cause? It has not. Instead, as we saw in some detail, Newton is only able to say *how much* "action" is at work *given a certain amount of deviation* of a body from uniform motion. Rational mechanics presupposes the existence of non-uniform curved motions to define impressed force in the first place. Coupled with the fact that impressed forces can only be measured with respect to these non-uniform motions, we begin to see the weakness of the picture of force as the *in itself* and motions as the *outward show*. In the actual practice of Newtonian science we only ever get our hands on force as a mirror image of motion, never as its cause.[17]

Seeing forces as causes and non-uniform motions as effects is built into the Newtonian picture from the outset. It is not something discovered in the course of the actual work of the *Principia*. And this point is only intensified by the establishment of gravity as a universal "cause." Once gravity is established as a relation between bodies and not as a force existing in bodies taken one by one, then motion cannot be separated from force as effect from cause. To say that bodies universally gravitate toward one another is just another way of saying that they *move* toward one another *in a certain way*. This "in a certain way" is the remarkable achievement of Newton's undertaking, for it establishes the precise character of what is uniform in the vast array of free motions of bodies in the cosmos. It discerns the law of these motions. But this uniformity cannot be maintained as the cause of the motions if a certain way of moving just is what universal gravitation is. We have certainly come to understand something about the world that we did not before following Newton's inquiry. But in reflecting on the over-

all character of the Newtonian project as a mode of knowing we must give up what we thought we were after—
the causes hiding behind appearances. Phenomena are not
the inessential appearing of a true but hidden world. The
apparent world is the true world.

"THE APPARENT WORLD is the true world." This does not
return us to the convictions of common sense. Common
sense does not distinguish an apparent from a true world.
Scientific consciousness—despite itself—has issued in the
thought that the distinction between an apparent and a true
world—a world *for us* that is *in itself* something else—cannot be maintained. But the thought that the apparent world
is in fact the true one can only abide if—in some way—the
distinction *is* maintained. And so it is. Even as we press scientific consciousness to give up its privileging of the hidden
world of forces over the apparent world of phenomena, we
do not doubt the explanatory power of its undertaking (as
long as we construe this explanatory power in terms of the
mathematical regularity of phenomena and not an explanation of cause and effect). Inasmuch as phenomena are intelligible, they cannot be regarded as merely something for
the senses. Scientific consciousness shows us one world that
is fully expressed as both sensible and intelligible.

THE WORLD is not the kind of thing scientific consciousness took it to be. What of its own activity? Scientific consciousness regarded itself as searching for the essential
beings hidden behind appearances. We can see that this
understanding of its activity is already undermined by the
simultaneous identity and difference of the true and apparent worlds. But we can see the same from another angle.

The Newtonian project can succeed only to the extent that its theoretical part is undertaken separately from its empirical part. The project of rational mechanics—once again—is to determine in principle the relationships between motions and forces. Newton is able to frame (the mathematical features of the motions in) possible worlds using pure thought alone. The explanatory satisfaction arrives when the results of theoretical world-making are brought to bear on empirical observations. When it is determined that a diversity of real motions can be comprehended under one law of force, we succeed in showing that one intelligible principle runs through a multiplicity of sensory phenomena. But it should be no surprise that what is discerned is an intelligible principle, for rational mechanics only ever dealt with intelligible things from the start.

The scientist scrutinizes phenomena and finds that bodies behave in the way that they would if they were moving under the influence of a certain law of force. In piercing the veil of appearances in order to find the true beings hidden underneath, the scientist finds only his own thoughts staring back. Being and thought are the same.

■

Scientific consciousness will be no happier with this conclusion than common sense was with the same proposal at the outset. In order to carry out its work, science has to disregard this conclusion. Its work of uncovering physical laws demands that it—at least implicitly—regards itself as getting its hands on the real substance of physical reality. That is, its work must be underpinned by a framework in which being is essential and thought is inessential.

And it will do no good for scientific consciousness to point to matter and motion and declare them to be what's really real. Holding up matter and motion as what is essential is only to revert back to the initial position of common sense. Matter and motion are just another way of saying *this here now*: all thises regarded as bits of matter; here and now extrapolated into the space and time implicit in motion. Furthermore, scientific consciousness would give up its own defining outlook in making such a claim. Only if the sensory exhibition of matter in motion is regarded as an outward expression of inward forces are we dealing with the scientific view of the world. And our exploration of Newton's work suggests that the mathematical character of the laws disclosed by natural science is a defining feature of this view. The mathematical specificity of the law of gravity, for instance, is just the kind of thing scientific consciousness is after.

THERE IS NO going back. The only way is forward. Scientific consciousness cannot follow us—it must stomach its internal contradictions as it carries on its work. But how are we to move forward?

The way forward might begin from a hesitation, or even profound disappointment, with the implications of "Being and thought are the same" as arrived at above. The sameness hit upon there is the sameness of the mathematical picture of the world constructed by rational mechanics and the lawful character of motions in the sensible world. But is this what the philosopher meant when saying thought and being are the same? Did it only have to do with the mathematical aspects of the motions of bodies? If nothing else, the thinness of this conclusion might spur us onward.

There is, though, another way to regard being and thought as the same in what we have been through. When the scientist finds his own thoughts behind the veil of appearances and when the apparent world is regarded as the truth of the inner world, we find that neither thought nor being are simple and self-same. Rather, both thought—in its search for confirmation of its own work in phenomena—and being—in the mirroring of the inward and outward *in each other*—share a different character. Both thought and being are wholes that differentiate themselves while remaining identical to themselves. This identity through difference is common to both.

Once we see *this* way in which thought and being are the same, new demands are made on our thinking. We will want to think more about the notion of a self-differentiating whole that nevertheless remains identical to itself. We will want to ponder the fact that this way of regarding the sameness of being and thought seems to keep them, in some way, distinct. Is this because there is a self-differentiating whole whose aspects *are* thought and being? Are thought and being the same *in* their difference? We will probably want to ask if our thinking has gone wildly astray with such questions!

But if we continue along these lines, we will see that the model of knowing in which essential being underwrites knowledge by our contingent minds has already been left behind.

We are no longer in the realm of common sense.

■

The whole of this chapter has been an effort to recapitulate, reflect on, and comprehend the three opening chapters of G. W. F. Hegel's *Phenomenology of Spirit*. If we have not mentioned Hegel or his book by name, or quoted passages from his text, our work has been no less an effort of reading than the other chapters in this book.

THE PHILOSOPHER Emmanuel Levinas, Lithuanian by birth and naturalized as a French citizen in 1931, spent nearly five years in a prisoner of war camp near Hanover, Germany, from June 1940 to April 1945. While imprisoned, Levinas worked on a short book, published in 1947 as *De l'existence à l'existant (Existence and Existents)*. In the opening pages of the book, Levinas sketches in striking fashion a central feature of our explorations of and with Plato, Aristotle, Kant, and Hegel. Levinas writes:

> The contact with light, the act of opening one's eyes, the lighting up of bare sensation, are apparently outside any relationship, and do not take up form like answers to questions. Light illuminates and is naturally understood; it is comprehension itself. But within this natural correlation between us and the world, in a sort of doubling back, a question arises, a being surprised by illumination. The wonder which Plato put at the origin of philosophy is an astonishment before the natural and intelligible. It is the very intelligibility of light that is astonishing; light is doubled up with a night. The astonishment does not arise out of a comparison with some order more natural than nature, but simply before intelligibility itself. (Trans. Alphonso Lingis [Dordrecht: Kluwer Academic Publishers, 1995], 22)

For all of its unusual questions, tangled arguments, and difficult verbiage, philosophy invites us to dwell within the astonishing space of intelligible luminosity that we call the world. The arduous character of philosophical reading should not blind us to the fact that philosophical thinking of the sort we have encountered in these pages begins and ends in the wonder occasioned by intelligibility itself.

Nevertheless, even this astonishment and wonder can be taken up by the radical questioning of the philosophical stance. The rest of Levinas' paragraph reads:

> Its strangeness is, we might say, due to its very reality, to the very fact there is existence. The questioning of being is an experience of being in its strangeness. It is then a way of taking up being. That is why the question about being—*What is being?*—has never been answered. There is no answer to being. It is absolutely impossible to envisage the direction in which that answer could have been sought. The question is itself a manifestation of the relationship with being. Being is essentially alien and strikes against us. We undergo its suffocating embrace like the night, but it does not respond to us. There is a pain in being. If philosophy is the questioning of being, it is already a taking on of being. And if it is more than this question, this is because it permits going beyond the question, and not because it answers it. What more there can be than the questioning of being is not some truth—but the good. (22–23)

Levinas' book goes on to explore being through a series of (perhaps) unexpected phenomena: fatigue, sleep, horror, appetite, insomnia. In the process, Levinas calls into question the primacy of the world of light for the philosopher.

What had seemed the natural starting point for philosophical inquiry becomes suspect. Levinas reminds us that nothing is safe from philosophical scrutiny.

THE APPREHENSION OF intelligible forms. The delineation of a determinate world. The experience of counting. Common sense. None of these are axioms, none provide a safe harbor for philosophical thought. Philosophical thinking is always open to—opens itself to—further questioning.

Hence the waking to eidetic insight, the deepening of worldly intelligibility in the quest for principles, the unfolding of mathematical thought into the grounds of conscious experience, and the overcoming of common sense are not indubitable conclusions of securely grounded inquiry. They are rather only moments in the never-finished task of philosophical thinking.

PAGE REFERENCES AND TRANSLATIONS

The page references for passages from Plato, Aristotle, and Kant correspond to the standard marginal pagination (Stephanus pagination in the case of Plato, Bekker for Aristotle, and the Akademie-Ausgabe in the case of Kant). Most modern editions of English translations of these works employ these pagination systems.

The translations I have used are listed below:

Plato

Gorgias, trans. Joe Sachs (Newburyport: Focus Publishing, 2009).

Meno, trans. George Anastaplo and Laurence Berns (Newburyport: Focus Publishing, 2004).

Phaedrus in *The Symposium and the Phaedrus: Plato's Erotic Dialogues*, trans. William S. Cobb (Albany: State University of New York Press, 1993).

Republic, trans. Allan Bloom (New York: Basic Books, 1968).

Theaetetus, trans. Joe Sachs (Newburyport: Focus Publishing, 2004).

Aristotle

Metaphysics, trans. Joe Sachs (Santa Fe: Green Lion Press, 1999).

Physics in *Aristotle's* Physics: *A Guided Study,* trans. Joe Sachs
(New Brunswick: Rutgers University Press, 1995).

Kant

Critique of Pure Reason, trans. Paul Guyer and Allen W. Wood
(Cambridge: Cambridge University Press, 1998).

GLOSSARY

The treatments of texts by Plato, Aristotle, Kant, and Hegel in this book do not presume that the reader is already familiar with these texts. For the most part, the texts considered do not rely on technical terms that require special definitions. (The outlier here is Kant, who makes extensive use of philosophical terms inherited from his predecessors.) I have tried to make clear the meanings of such terms as they are encountered. Nevertheless, the reader may find the reminders gathered here helpful in navigating words and usages that fall outside of ordinary speech. The entries are organized according to the preceding chapters.

Wakefulness

form (*eidos*)   The literal meaning of the word points to the "look" of something. *Eidos* is a noun derived from the verb to see. We can discriminate some things by sight because different things look different, have different looks. For such things, form would pertain to those visible aspects that allow something to be recognized as the kind of thing that it is. ("*What is that?*" "*It* looks *like a dog.*") In this way, *eidos* also comes to mean class, kind, or type—things of the same kind share a look. Plato's Socrates extends the scope of this word to things that are not visible, for instance, virtue, knowledge, and goodness. Socrates often asks his interlocutors to search for the looks of such things. These looks would be apprehended not with eyes, but with intellect. In the *Republic*, Socrates says that the philosopher is the person who is capable of and takes delight in apprehending forms of this kind.

sensible/intelligible The notion of forms as the looks of non-visible things carries with it the distinction between the sensible and the intelligible. If there are objects that can only be apprehended by the intellect, then the world cannot be reduced to what is taken in through the senses.

analogizomai/sullogismos Both of these Greek words carry into English a similar meaning, a kind of reckoning by gathering things together. The notion of reckoning or calculation is brought to both words through the common root *logizomai*, itself rooted in *logos*, which means both speech and reason. The prefixes of the words indicate, however, a difference in how such reckoning might take place. The *ana-* of *analogizomai* suggests an up-and-down, or back-and-forth, movement. We perform this kind of movement in thought when making comparisons. (Note the connection between analogy and *analogizomai*.) For *sullogismos*, the prefix *sul-* indicates a binding together. The Greek word is carried directly into English as syllogism, a yoking together of premises in order to draw a conclusion.

incommensurable In its mathematical meaning, incommensurable refers to magnitudes for which there is no common measure. It can be proven, for example, that there is no common measure for the side and diagonal of a square. That is, while the side of a square can be divided into ever smaller proper parts—equal parts that fit exactly onto the side—no such part can measure out exactly the diagonal of that square. Incommensurable translates the

Greek word *alogon*, which means unsayable, without reason, or incapable of reckoning.

World

contradiction   A contradiction can occur in speech when we say both something and its opposite. When Aristotle claims that contradictions are impossible, he does not mean that we cannot contradict ourselves in what we say. His claim is about things and states of affairs. This is why the principle contains the qualifications "at the same time" and "in the same respect." It is possible for it to be both day and night in one place, but not at the same time. It is possible for it to be both day and night at the same time, but not in the same respect: it is day *here*, but night *there*. Contradictions in speech point to impossible conditions in the world.

determinate/determination   These are not Aristotle's words, but are used throughout the chapter to indicate the set of problems Aristotle takes up, problems pertaining to the question of being. The question of being must first face the question of whether it is right to ask *what* a thing is. If one is justified in asking this question, then things must be determined in some way. There must be some specifiable ways in which a thing is what it is. This is related to contradiction: if something is determinate, then it is limited; to be determinately *this* is to *not be that*.

essential/incidental   In asking *what* something is we imply that the thing has determinations. But we can also ask whether all determinations answer the *what* question in the same way. We can ask whether a particular determination is essential to what something is, such that without that determination the thing would no longer be itself; or whether that determination could change and the thing would remain—in some crucial way—the same thing (despite the change).

material/form   Aristotle maintains that perceptible/bodily things can be scrutinized in terms of material and form. This distinction is not self-evident, but is pressed upon us from a number of directions. Two in particular are central to questions taken up in the chapter. First, ordinary experience shows that one and the same thing is capable of gradual change. Aristotle asserts that such change occurs between a pair of contraries. For example, a shirt on a clothesline passes (by degrees) from wet to dry. But it is not the wet that becomes dry, but some "underlying thing." We can call this underlying thing "material." Second, things that are capable of this kind of change often admit of two basic kinds of description, one that says what a thing is *made from*, and one that says what *kind* of thing it is. The item on the clothesline is made from cotton cloth, but the kind of thing that it is is a shirt.

motion/rest   Aristotle knows that things can move from one place to another, and that when they are not moving in this way that they remain in the same place. But this is not what motion and rest primarily mean for Aristotle. In its principal sense, motion names the state of a thing that is *on the way* to being something while *not yet* being that. This means that genuine motions are never random occurrences, but contain their endpoints in themselves. In turn, rest is not understood as the absence of motion, but as its fulfillment. The paradigm of motion is the growth and maturation of an organism. The newly-born organism *moves toward* the mature thing it is meant to be and *comes to rest* in the life it leads as that mature thing.

ousia   This is the central word of Aristotle's metaphysics. It is a form of the verb "to be" and is carried into philosophical usage from its ordinary usage, where it indicates one's possessions in the broad sense. The first meaning given in the Greek lexicon is "that which is one's own, one's substance, property." Aristotle wants to know, for any given thing, what its *own* is, what belongs most properly to it, what makes it the thing that it is. This is why he says that the question of being is the question of *ousia*.

Sum

a priori The literal meaning of the Latin is "from what comes before." Kant's use of the term does not indicate temporal priority, but rather priority in principle. Kant calls our forms of intuition and the categories of the understanding a priori because they "come before" empirical experience in that they make experience possible. Certain activities and products of the mind can also be called a priori if they engage only the a priori faculties of the mind. (For instance, mathematical propositions are called a priori since they do not rely on experience for either their content or their form.) See TRANSCENDENTAL and PURE.

appearance All objects of empirical experience are said by Kant to be appearances. This is meant to contrast with our sense that we have contact with things as they are in themselves. Kant asserts that his predecessors had not been able to explain how empirical knowledge is possible because philosophers had held that knowledge must be obtained by adjusting the mind to the way that things are in themselves. Kant turns this way of looking at things around and maintains that the objects of empirical experience are made possible in the first place by the character of our forms of intuition and understanding. The term appearance is thus meant to draw a boundary: experience is *only* of appearances, never of things in themselves. See INTUITION.

category This is the name given by Kant to the pure (or a priori) concepts of the mind. See A PRIORI, CONCEPT, PURE, and UNDERSTANDING.

concept A concept is that which brings unity to a judgment; this unity is accomplished by bringing one concept under another. We "comprehend" one concept in terms of another. In the judgment "Some roses are red" nothing unified is thought by "Some roses," according to Kant, until that representation is brought under the concept red. Most of our concepts are derived from experience, but some, Kant says, we possess a priori. See A PRIORI, CATEGORY, REPRESENTATION, and UNDERSTANDING.

consciousness In one sense, the term consciousness indicates any activity of the mind: perceiving, thinking, imagining, wishing, willing, etc. In another sense, consciousness is none of these activities in particular, but a kind of view on them, the ability to be aware that one is perceiving, thinking, imagining, wishing, or willing. For Kant this means that consciousness implies self-consciousness.

critique When Kant call his book a critique, he means something rather particular: an investigation of the limits of our knowledge. The determination of the limits of possible knowledge, however, is not done by investigating the objects of our knowledge directly, but by scrutinizing our own powers for knowing. In this sense, critique does not carry a negative connotation; it indicates only a discerning scrutiny of pure reason. Nevertheless, this scrutiny shows us why reason is prone to overstep its proper boundaries, and so critique can also be heard in its more derogatory sense, as criticism.

intuition Kant says that we possess two basic mental powers. One power is the capacity for receiving objects; the other is the power of thinking. The receptive power Kant calls intuition. Space and time are the forms of intuition, meaning they are the forms in which anything we receive in experience must be received. One should not hear in this term the usual meaning in colloquial English: understanding something immediately or unconsciously, or understanding something through feeling. See APPEARANCE and UNDERSTANDING.

judgment   For Kant, the fundamental activity of the mind is the forming of judgments. A judgment can be expressed as a sentence, but is not itself a sentence. If I say "This rose is red" and mean it, I both utter a sentence and make a judgment. The judgment, properly speaking, is the "putting together" of rose and red by the mind. The "is" in the sentence indicates that the mind is attaching redness to the rose. Kant calls the things brought together in a judgment concepts. See CONCEPT.

pure   The term pure should be heard in contrast to empirical. Empirical experience requires that we be affected by something outside us. But since Kant's view of human cognition maintains that we have mental powers of intuition and understanding that are not derived from experience, those powers are able to operate independently of what is given to experience. (For instance, in doing mathematics.) Both the activities and products of thinking that are independent from experience are called pure. See A PRIORI and TRANSCENDENTAL.

receptivity   see INTUITION.

representation   This term can refer to all things that are either given to or can be brought before the mind, for instance, sensations, perceptions, concepts, and images.

schematism/schema   While Kant maintains that knowledge and experience require both intuition and concepts, he recognizes that some explanation must be given about how intuitions and concepts can be brought together. The power by which this bringing-together is effected he calls schematism, while admitting that its operation remains obscure. We get some sense of its work in name itself: the product of schematism is a schema, a "shape." Schematism sketches the "shape" of a concept in intuition.

transcendental   Kant holds that in order to comprehend ordinary experience we must "cross over" from our usual understanding of experience to a consideration of the very conditions of experience. We must move, as it were, from experience as a fact to what experience in principle requires. Ordinary experience must, in this sense, be "transcended." But the transcendental principles of experience are not "transcendent," if by that we would mean they exist in some other realm or bring us into contact with non-empirical beings. The transcendental principles of ordinary experience only have meaning with respect to the experiences they make possible. See A PRIORI and PURE.

understanding   Understanding is the name given to our power to form judgments. This power can be viewed on the one hand as an activity: when we are judging we are understanding. It can also be viewed as the possessor of concepts: judging must take place by bringing concepts together, and so the mind must have concepts at its disposal. Kant argues that the understanding possesses certain a priori concepts, which he calls categories. See CONCEPT, INTUITION, and JUDGMENT.

Thought/Being

certainty/truth   When we claim to know something, that claim is accompanied by a conviction of certainty. This certainty is a feature of the experience of knowing. (Without it, we restrict ourselves to claims of belief, opinion, or conjecture.) But being certain that we know something is no guarantee that we are right. Being right would require the content of our conviction to be true. The test for truth entails matching up what we are certain about with our understanding of what makes knowledge possible at all.

immediate/mediated The certainty in knowing is immediate, direct; it is the starting point in the experience of knowing. Certainty is always correlated with another claim about immediacy, that there is something direct and unmediated that we are in contact with. (In the chapter, there are three versions of this kind of immediacy: direct contact with particular objects, direct contact with the properties of objects, and the direct manifestation of force in sense qualities.) Both kinds of immediacy turn out to be illusory: the experience of immediate certainty and the sense that the world is immediately available in fact pass through—are mediated by—our thoughts about how the world hangs together.

particular/universal We encounter the world as a world of particulars, that is, unique and singular things: this object here and that one there; this patch of color in front of me and that sound coming from behind me. It seems that particulars are immediately present to us, that they are the real ground of what makes up the world and what makes experience of the world possible. Universals—general terms—seem to only come after. "Here" and "there," "this" and "that," we believe, are just words that we attach to particulars. (The same would be the case with most other words. Only proper names could be adequate to particularity.) Scrutiny of our experience of particulars, however, suggests that the apparent primacy and immediacy of particulars is always mediated by universals, that the world itself depends—in some way—on general terms.

force   The scientific view of the world and our knowledge of it does not hold that we have immediate access to what is true in the world. It asserts, rather, that there is something at work behind what is apprehended by sense perception, something real but not itself sensible. Force is a name for this something.

NOTES

Wakefulness

1. The *Republic* is a so-called reported dialogue, that is, the text as a whole is in the voice of one person recounting a conversation that has already taken place. The *Republic* is reported by Socrates. (The dialogue begins, "I went down to the Piraeus yesterday with Glaucon . . .") In the quotation that follows "he" is Glaucon and the first speaker is Socrates.

2. See *Republic* 357c.

3. Just before offering the definition of the philosopher with which we began, Socrates had already asserted that philosophers were those who have desire for every sort of learning. Glaucon finds this strange, since it seems to him that everyone who loves taking things in through the senses (say, a music lover) would be a philosopher. Socrates' statement about love of the sight of the truth is meant to distinguish the philosopher's desire from these others. That distinguishing continues in what follows.

4. In the *Phaedo*, Socrates does say that he is in the practice of *hypothesizing* forms. He also says that this hypothesizing is "artless" and that assertions such as "Just actions are just because they partake of justice" don't really tell us anything. As we will see, this apparent discrepancy arises from the fact that it is not clear that Socrates is a philosopher in the sense we are now considering. What we can say for now, again, is that if the philosopher has a genuine vision of forms, then statements like

the one about just things and justice would spring from (a special kind of) knowledge. (See *Phaedo*, 100d–102a.)

5. I will not attempt to explicitly argue *against* the accusation made by Polus, that Socrates is divisive in his way of questioning people. This is a complex issue and I would not want to deny simply that Socrates does such things. For now, I wish only to take Socrates at his word in his exchanges with Polus and measure their conversation against how Socrates goes on to characterize that conversation.

6. We will not remark upon the past/present/future part of Theaetetus' answer. It seems partly grounded in an earlier part of the dialogue between Socrates and Theodorus. I think it might suffice for now to see that what Theaetetus wants to point to has to do with ordinary human experience.

7. One might ask at this point for it to be shown that there can be such squares. This is readily done on the basis of a proposition from Book II of Euclid's *Elements*. It is shown in proposition II.14 that a square can be constructed equal (in area) to any rectilinear figure. Construction of a rectilinear figure equal to any area represented by a whole number can be easily obtained by an arrangement of unit squares.

8. For a brief discussion of incommensurability and a proof that the side and diagonal of a square are incommensurable, see Thomas L. Heath, *The Thirteen Books of Euclid's Elements, Volume 3* (New York: Dover, 1956), 1–4 and 18–20.

9. That is, the lines on which squares are built.

10. Here, as throughout this chapter, I am not endeavoring to provide commentary on the dialogue under consideration. In this case, for example, there is a long playful speech between Meno's initial question and Socrates' question about needing to know what virtue is before looking into how it is acquired. Careful scrutiny of the intervening speech cannot be omitted if one aims to read the dialogue as a whole.

World

1. In using this phrase to designate "human being," Aristotle does not seem to be suggesting that it is an *adequate* designation of what a human being is.

2. For his larger project in the *Physics*, the inclusion of the simple bodies and the discussion of how they are by nature are important. We will leave them aside and focus on living things.

3. We will also leave aside things that are "put together" by chance and contrast plants and animals with man-made items.

4. Again, leaving aside the possibility of such things coming together by chance. Even if we ignore the unlikelihood of a bed made from wood, glue, and nails being formed by chance, a bed made by chance is not the same as a bed made from art even if the two beds happen to be physically identical. The beds would still differ in their source of change.

5. See chapters 6 and 7 of *Le Monde*.

6. How one should conceive of motion as a quantity and what sort of quantity is actually conserved in physical phenomena is one of the fascinating stories that unfolds in modern science. Important early moves in this story can be found in works by Descartes, Huygens, Newton, and Leibniz, but the questions persist and are further developed in the treatment of energy in the 19th century.

7. What exactly a physical law is and how it should be conceived also has a vexed history. One does not find particularly robust discussions in the works of early modern science themselves. In fact, it is in philosophical works such as Kant's *Critique of Pure Reason* where the question is given a proper treatment. (Proper not because Kant's account is the right one, but because his book shows how deep the question goes and how much is at stake in answering it.) Classical and contemporary philosophy of science has wrestled with this question without coming to any clear answer.

8. There is another complicated story concerning relative motion. A limited conception of the relativity of motion underwrites the kinematics and mechanics of the late 17th century and is either implicit or explicit in the works of Galileo, Huygens, and Newton. This limited conception is restricted to uniform motions in straight lines. Any body moving at a constant speed in a straight line can be considered to be at rest.

Whether such a body is moving or resting can be considered, as it were, a matter of perspective. Famously, Newton considered curved and accelerated motions to be non-relative (i.e., they contain some "absolute" aspect). The coherence of Newton's arguments for absolute motion were subsequently questioned by various thinkers and were ultimately refuted by Einstein's general theory of relativity.

9. Whether the coherence of such a scenario would hold up under further scrutiny is another matter. I only want to suggest that this kind of extrinsic but non-incidental source and cause is logically conceivable in this narrow way.

10. We will skip over the first paragraph of the chapter and return to it after looking at the rest of the chapter and a detour through the *Physics*.

11. As always, qualifications may be required. In some cases, as with red wines that contain sediment, one might ask for a new bottle to be opened rather than take what remains in the bottle your host has been pouring from.

12. The terms here follow Aristotle's ways of speaking, not the modern taxonomic terminology.

13. A view of the world in terms of genus categories seems to me a non-starter. We saw above that the genus terms seem not to operate independently of the smaller categories below them. Genus terms seem to *imply* discrete individuals in a way that basic physical substrates do not.

14. See *An Intermediate Greek-English Lexicon* (Oxford: Oxford University Press, 1889), 579.

15. There are, of course, circumstances when the phrase "many waters" might be fitting, for example, if we were sampling the taste of waters from different natural springs. But here the manyness is of a different sort from the manyness of horses in a field. It is closer to something like "There are many species in the garden," which points not to a multitude of individual plants but to a multitude of *types*.

16. Aristotle's principal example in this section is the production of health, but he mentions house building a number of times alongside of medicine. I have extrapolated some of what he says about medicine to house building.

17. As usual, there is some flexibility here. One might at first be tempted to say that a house is primarily a thing that provides shelter. But we might then go further and say that the sheltering provided by a house is in service of the house as a place to cultivate living well, which would exceed mere sheltering. We can also see how we might find houses put to aberrant or degenerative uses, say, as displays of wealth.

Sum

1. There are predicates that do apply only to bodies, but since they are narrower in scope than "all bodies" they cannot be used to think something about all bodies. For instance, bodies can be round, but the sentence "All bodies are round" is false, not only as a matter of fact, as it were, but as a matter of form. Since the predicate is narrower than the subject, it cannot be true. The only universal judgment where the predicate is equal in scope to the subject is the one where the subject is repeated in the predicate ("All bodies are bodies"), but nothing is *thought* in such a judgment.

2. As an *empirical* concept, I must learn about mallet-marks through experience.

3. This way of putting it is still pretty clumsy. Even when painted black, there will likely be subtle visual clues of sheen and texture that signal that the black thing is painted wood rather than rubber. But these visual clues have their own mediating concepts.

4. A less idiomatic form of these judgments makes the number-as-predicate point clearer: "The apples are 23," "The rows are 23."

5. Our examples have all been categorical judgments, ones of the form "S is P," where S has either been an "all" or a "this." These two types of judgments are called universal and singular; universal in the first case because the judgment covers every member of a multitude; singular in the second because the judgment makes an assertion about only one object. There is a third type of categorical judgment, particular judgments, that bring part of a multitude under a concept; for instance, "Some pieces of metal are copper."

6. Note that in talking about a field of color as given, there seems already to be some unity in the given. We will see the significance of this below.

7. Just to be clear, the words "intuition" and "intuitive" mark out the domain of givenness and receptivity in cognition. It would be misleading to hear in these terms their typical meanings in colloquial English: understanding things immediately or unconsciously, or understanding things through feeling.

8. In fact, Kant says it is an "infinite given magnitude." Establishing the infiniteness of space will not be essential for our purposes; seeing it as given will suffice. One way to understand why Kant claims space is given as infinite is to see that any space that can be imagined must be imagined as itself contained within—as being a part of—the one given space. This does not mean that we can imagine the infiniteness of space all at once, only that our imagining of finite spaces are, as it were, themselves always contained by a boundless space.

9. "Begin from" because experience in one sense is nothing but a "stream of consciousness." But one might notice the enormous question lurking here, for even if it is the case that consciousness comes in a stream, the order of events I encounter is not regarded as being determined by me (in contrast to the events I initiate). Rather, experience includes the conviction that certain events happen in some particular order. *I* see them occurring in a certain order *because* they happen in that order. This necessity of an objective ordering of events in time is one of the central problems of the first portion of the *Critique of Pure Reason*. We can note at this point that Kant's explanation of objective time order is not based on time itself; that is, coming-one-after-another, as a form of ordering representations, cannot be the ground of whether one event must have come before another. Such a ground must be one that can provide a reason for the necessary time order. Hence, any necessity in the temporal order of events must be searched for in the understanding and not in our forms of receptivity.

10. Hence, we can see that something like our thought experiment of subtracting the "matter" of sensation to yield a given space as a form of ordering needs to be qualified ret-

rospectively. It turns out that we *cannot* have any introspective access to space *purely* as a form of receptivity since in our introspection we seem to encounter a space that is already unified by productive synthesis of the imagination.

11. This, we might say, is a psychological fact, but not yet a transcendental principle.

12. In principle, not in time.

13. Hopefully it is clear, however, that such real principles, for Kant, are not *transcendent immaterial beings*. The real/ideal parallax would be swept away if they were. Thus pure synthesis is the real basis of empirical consciousness, but simultaneously ideal in that it has no import outside of empirical experience. Hence pure synthesis cannot be equated with an immaterial soul, which could be construed as a being that has some real standing independently from possible experience.

14. Two limitations of what we can accomplish here should be noted. First, we will not attempt to delve into the nature of Kant's "deduction" of our possession of pure concepts. Indeed, even understanding what he means by deduction is thorny. It will suffice to note that this deduction has the general character of the other instances of transcendental reflection that we have considered; that is, it would have to be shown that without our possession of pure concepts experience would be impossible. Second, we will not endeavor to introduce the full "table of categories" that contains these pure concepts. Nor will we venture to indicate how these pure concepts are related to various forms of judgments. This second pair of limitations means that we will not attempt to explore how experience as a whole is made possible by pure concepts. Why this is the case can be seen if we consider that ordinary experience (as mentioned in a previous note) includes an objective ordering of time. This feature of experience is dependent on the pure concept of a cause, and this pure concept is one of those we will not take up.

15. This helps explain why for Kant intellect is at bottom a power of spontaneity. We do not (in the usual sense) consciously—that is, deliberately—employ pure concepts. Consciousness *happens* through the spontaneous employment of pure concepts.

16. Note that as with our treatment of numerical and geometric magnitudes above, unity, plurality, and totality imply one another. For instance, the singular judgment "This is an apple" is meaningful only if judgments of the form "Some apples are X" and "All apples are Y" are possible. If they weren't, "apple" would not be a real concept but only a proper name.

Thought/Being

1. This paragraph is a brief indication of how what is true on the side of the object for consciousness is doubled in consciousness' view of its own activity. (In this case, both the object and "I" are shown to lack the determinateness consciousness regards them as having.) Our emphasis in what follows will fall on the side of objects, although at certain moments we will see how things look in terms of the activity of consciousness as well.

2. Hence even if common sense fails to acknowledge the mediation of its awareness of particular things through its presuppositions about *this here now* (as was discussed above), it will still end up having to abandon its claim of immediate knowing of particulars if it shifts ground to knowledge through properties.

3. The need for scare quotes will be made clear as we proceed. The received truism is that Newton discovers that gravity is the cause of objects falling to the ground by means of a force of attraction. What goes overlooked in the truism is that it doesn't take a Newton to know that objects are "attracted" to the ground. This is in no need of discovery. The precise character of the *explanation* of the nature of this attraction is what is novel in Newton's work. Hence part of our work ahead will be to understand how mathematical physics goes about explaining aspects of ordinary experience and why "discovery" is an inapt term to capture its work.

4. The following pages will reconstruct in some detail the main line of argument in Newton's book. The length and amount of detail in these pages may strike some readers as unwarranted. My goal in providing this detail is to allow us sufficient opportunity to see how scientific consciousness fails

to make good on its larger goals both from within its own specific projects and despite the explanatory success of its efforts. Without working through the concepts, reasoning, evidence, and results of some such undertaking we will not be able to see clearly how the failure of scientific consciousness to raise its certainty to truth is *immanent* within the parameters of its own thinking. Page references are to Isaac Newton, *The Principia: Mathematical Principles of Natural Philosophy*, trans. I. Bernard Cohen and Anne Whitman (Berkeley: University of California Press, 1999).

5. And, strictly speaking, such "amounts" cannot be specified in absolute terms. Newton's propositions always express amounts of force as proportions: change of motion A : change of motion B :: amount of force X : amount of force Y.

6. We probably cannot say too many times that the presence of forces *as such* in the world is not proven in Newton's book. The world as a play of forces is the *presupposed framework* for this manner of investigating nature.

7. Newton's proofs rely on the Laws of Motion, which follow the definitions at the beginning of the treatise, and on the mathematics developed in the Lemmas (Newton's version of the calculus). While both the Laws and Lemmas are worthy of close study, their precise character is not central to the story we want to follow. It is enough to understand that the proofs we will consider rest on a purely theoretical foundation and are not dependent on empirical observations.

8. That is, if the *ratio* of the square of the periodic time to the cube of the radius is constant for all bodies moving uniformly in a circle around the same center.

9. While he makes it clear that the central goal of the *Principia* is to determine the causes of celestial motions, Newton seems to go out of his way to show that rational mechanics is not limited to the study of real-world motions. Proposition 9 is an example. In this proposition Newton considers a certain kind of spiral motion with a fixed center. He shows that the force required for this motion would vary as the *cube* of the distance from the center. Even if no such motion has or will ever be observed, rational mechanics can show what species of

force would be at work if there were really a body moving in this way.

10. Kepler's first law states that the shape of the planetary orbits is elliptical. This is not incidental to Newton's work in the *Principia* and, indeed, Newton is able to show that bodies that move in ellipses require a force that varies inversely as the square of distance. But as we will see, the argument in Book III for universal gravitation can proceed without bringing in the elliptical character of orbits. Partly this is the case because the orbits of the planets and the moons of Jupiter and Saturn are close enough to being circular that Proposition 4 can carry the burden of the argument.

11. I skip over here the important subtleties of what might be entailed in establishing empirical facts. For instance, Kepler himself determines the law of equal areas by showing that predictive calculations *based on* the law are very accurate. The equal areas are not "directly" observed. But it is important to see that such complications of empirical fact gathering are different in kind from rational mechanics. In the first case, one is only dealing with *descriptive* features of the motion; in the second case, one infers, in principle, relations of cause and effect.

12. Again, this way of looking at the matter is the result of having decomposed the curved orbit of the moon into two straight-line motions. If we put the two motions back together, we find that the 16 feet that the moon "falls" toward the earth in a minute combines with the sideways motion of the moon to keep the moon (roughly) at a constant distance from the earth. One can think of it this way: if the moon didn't "fall" toward the earth, it would fly off into space and never come back.

13. He has to do this in a somewhat different manner than with the solar planets and the moons of Jupiter and Saturn, since our moon has no companion satellites by which to establish the $\frac{3}{2}$ power relationship.

14. It is a happy accident that the numbers work out so nicely here. The 16 feet that both bodies fall are the result of uniformly accelerated motion from rest. (Imagine holding a ball in your hand and letting it go.) The calculation that determines how far a body will fall from rest involves squaring the

time. Since the falling of the moon is calculated for a minute, this minute is equal to 60×60 seconds when squared. Hence when we scale from minutes to seconds in determining the amount of fall at the surface of the earth, the 60×60 increase in the strength of the centripetal force is counterbalanced by the 60×60 diminishment in the square of the time. This accounts for the equal distance of freefall in one minute at the distance of the moon and one second at the surface of the earth.

15. The picture that emerges—contrary to ordinary intuition—is one in which not only are falling bodies and moons and planets understood as being attracted to other bodies (for instance, the moon *to* the earth), but those other bodies must now be understood as being attracted to the falling and revolving bodies. When a stone falls to earth, it is not just that a force is acting on the stone in the direction of the center of the earth. As a mutual attraction, the force impressed on the stone is matched by a force ("equal and opposite") impressed on the earth.

16. The development of natural science after Newton *is*, at times, very much a matter of assessing whether his work is sufficiently explanatory. That is, those following Newton want to know the extent to which the principles derived in his work do in fact fit with phenomena. In small and large ways, Newton's work is adjusted and ultimately overturned by those who come after him. But these adjustments and overturnings are done from within the framework of scientific consciousness. That is, they share with Newton the basic picture of where truth resides and how to find it. In the remainder of this chapter, we will not be concerned with whether Newton has the right scientific account of free motion in the cosmos, but with whether the understanding of truth entailed in the *kind* of endeavor Newton exemplifies is sound.

17. Consider the familiar formulation: force *equals* mass × acceleration.

CPSIA information can be obtained
at www.ICGtesting.com
Printed in the USA
LVHW032236030619
620021LV00002B/2